"FAITH MUST BE TESTED. IF IT IS UNBROKEN, THEN IT IS NOT WHOLE … BUT IT MUST NOT REMAIN SEVERED OR SUNDERED. WE MUST PRESS ON, FACING UP TO WHAT HAPPENED IN THE PAST AND WHAT IS HAPPENING IN THE WORLD TODAY.
— *ELIE WIESEL*

**To my father, Leon Weber, and to all of us
who long to see our fathers again.**

Learning to Jump Again

A Memoir of Grief and Hope

Anthony Weber

WestBow
PRESS
A DIVISION OF THOMAS NELSON

WestBow Press books may be ordered through booksellers or by contacting:

WestBow Press
A Division of Thomas Nelson
1663 Liberty Drive
Bloomington, IN 47403
www.westbowpress.com
1-(866) 928-1240

Because of the dynamic nature of the Internet, any web addresses or links contained in this book may have changed since publication and may no longer be valid. The views expressed in this work are solely those of the author and do not necessarily reflect the views of the publisher, and the publisher hereby disclaims any responsibility for them.

Any people depicted in stock imagery provided by Thinkstock are models, and such images are being used for illustrative purposes only.

Certain stock imagery © Thinkstock.

ISBN: 978-1-4497-2130-5 (sc)
ISBN: 978-1-4497-2131-2 (hc)
ISBN: 978-1-4497-2129-9 (e)

Library of Congress Control Number: 2011912198

Printed in the United States of America

WestBow Press rev. date: 08/03/2011

Contents

FROM HEART TO HEAD

My dad died at age fifty-seven after battling pancreatic cancer for two and a half years.

In a world increasingly full of absentee fathers and men stuck in suspended adolescence, my grandpa raised a son who was neither of those. Leon Weber was a good man and a good father, and I loved him.

After he died, I started a journal. Though originally I used it as an intensely private outlet for the emotional upheaval that followed my father's burial, I decided to share my journey with others instead of staying withdrawn. When I posted a number of entries on Facebook, the unexpected responses overwhelmed me.

Friends and strangers poured out raw, primal thoughts and emotions that they had never expressed freely before. I realized then that this journal could be helpful in at least starting people on a path toward freedom and healing.

This is my journey through the valleys and the shadows; it is from my perspective only. It is not a standard for others; it is not a document that reveals my better moments. I am not proud of everything I felt (and still feel, for that matter), but if this journal is helpful, I'm okay with showing a side of my nature that I was once more comfortable keeping hidden.

I would like to provide connection and commiseration for all of us who grieve, but I don't want it to finish there. To that end, I have included some chapters with more objective insights (personal and biblical) to balance the raw emotiveness of the journal. In addition, there are several essays at the end that delve more deeply into the philosophical and theological problem of pain in the world.

There are no isolated stories.

May we find comfort together.

FRODO: "I WISH THE RING HAD NEVER COME TO ME. I WISH NONE OF THIS HAD HAPPENED."

GANDALF: "SO DO ALL WHO LIVE TO SEE SUCH TIMES. BUT THAT IS NOT FOR THEM TO DECIDE. ALL WE HAVE TO DECIDE IS WHAT TO DO WITH THE TIME THAT IS GIVEN TO US."

—J. R. R. Tolkien, *The Fellowship of the Ring*

THE SITUATION

SITUATION: A COMPLEX OR CRITICAL CONDITION
OR POSITION IN WHICH YOU FIND YOURSELF.

"We didn't make the world. All we have to do is live in it."
—Stephen R. Donaldson

Fall 2000

When my dad drove from Columbus to my house in Traverse City in October, he was yellow, a deep-to-the-depth-of-his-soul color that made the entire world seem sick.

I knew even then the truth was more than he and my mom stoically claimed. Time trickled away as the doctor misdiagnosed the cause of his jaundice. "He drank some bad imported tea," the doctor said. But my parents didn't buy it. The grass was meant to be green; the sky was meant to be blue; my house was meant to be whatever color I had inappropriately painted it at that time. My dad was *not* meant to be yellow. "A breech in nature," said Macbeth, speaking of the rightful king's mortal wounds. I could not force myself to look at him directly for much of that weekend, even though they visited for three days. I wish I had been strong enough to watch, but I looked away even as the colors of nature conspired to betray my father. My dad, mom, and sister had come for the color tour in Michigan, and that made sense. In the fall, leaves turn yellow, and this change is part of the cycle of life, both beautiful and good. When we all returned from our scenic drive, Dad stood with me on my back deck, but I could not look at him. Now, because of the fall, it was my dad who turned yellow; it was part of the cycle of death; and it was awful and cruel.

A friend stopped by that weekend to borrow some tools, and I stammered through an explanation of why my visiting father was yellow. My friend looked at me gently but said nothing. His son had been killed in a traffic accident not so long before. He knew that after the fall comes winter, and after the chill comes the cold, and he was mercifully silent.

My dad grew up a conservative Mennonite dairy farmer in Lancaster County, Pennsylvania. Mom spoke Pennsylvania Dutch before she spoke English, and Dad understood every word. Farms and farm markets? Check. (Mom and Dad met at a farm market called the Green Dragon, which seems like an odd name for a place where Mennonites sold stuff, but on with the checklist.)

> *Plain clothes? Check. One time, when Dad went to the store to get powdered milk for the calves, he asked for "hommy" powder, baffling the store manager until an Amish farmer explained what he meant.*

When the jaundice diagnosis morphed into a cancer diagnosis, many people thought God had to heal him. For various reasons, God couldn't let him die; God needed him here on earth; God had given them a magical wand, a verse that they could wave over his yellow skin. Dozens of people called my parents to assure them that "God has given me a Word." The verse, "You shall have none of these diseases," magically left its Hebraic, post-Egyptian context and landed just a bit off Broad Street. It was a typical verse-bite, full of nothing but happy thoughts. Two thumbs up for the power of positive thinking. Nobody called with, "The Lord gives and the Lord takes away. Blessed be His name." Job had apparently been banished from the canon of promises. In fact, a friend (one of Job's twenty-first-century friends, perhaps?) has since explained to me how God's rebuttal at the end of the book rebuked Job for that pithy statement. "Just pray and trust God." That sentence I heard more times than I care to recount. But the universe does not operate by the secret; even if it did, I am not the secret keeper. I am not God's master. He is not a tame lion, said C. S. Lewis, and none of us are lion tamers anyway.

As the prognosis grew even grimmer, the news that God did not share the perspective of the verse-biters seemed to surprise people. "It's still nothing to worry about. Your dad is confident it will be okay." Of course he was. He had to be, and I don't blame him. Those closest to him had to be positive, and it was good and right that they were. If the skin and the soul are connected, then positive thoughts sometimes equal positive results.

I, on the other hand, did not live near him. I did not have to be outwardly or inwardly confident, and I was neither. Those who lived with and near him had to bear that burden. *It's no use to worry,* I told myself, as if that would help. But who was I kidding? The source of my life had changed his color, like a chameleon. When he rested on a vibrant tree of life, he blended in and looked alive; now that he perched on a shriveled, dying tree, blending in once again, what was I to conclude? He was shedding his skin and turning into something different. Before, he was neither yellow, nor gaunt, nor full of cancer, and he was alive. Now the first three had changed; what to do with the fourth? Were there really that many other options? The corruptible must be shed before we can put on the incorruptible. There is no other way. I felt like I was the only one praying, "Lord, I believe. Help my unbelief." Did anyone else remember that Jesus said, "My God, why have you forsaken me?" Was it true that if I mustered enough faith and prayed hard enough, God would have to heal my father? We needed only a mustard seed's worth of faith. Apparently, none of us possessed even that much.

There is an insecurity that comes with sickness, especially an illness that can't be seen or predicted. When I hurt my knees playing basketball, the doctor diagnosed my injury, fixed my joints, and then gave me a timetable for healing: "In six months you will be pain-free. And enjoy the Darvocet."

> "Be true, Unbeliever."
> —Stephen R. Donaldson

Cancer is a little more vague. I know someone with bladder cancer. This cancer has a pretty clear diagnosis; a fairly successful fix is possible, perhaps even probable, even if it's no fun. The timetable and quality of life, however, remain unclear. He will likely stop peeing blood, but will he be able to work? To enjoy his family? To be pain-free?

With pancreatic cancer, the insecurity comes before the diagnosis— "Why is he yellow?" My family and I spent an hour talking with the surgeon one afternoon, and while we all tried to be optimistic, we learned something that day. The only thing up in the air after this diagnosis was whether Dad had six months or five years to live. The only uncertainty lay in the timing. Barring an act of God, Dad would die.

*For more on <u>Confronting Life Honestly</u>, see page 84.

THE ESCALATION

ESCALATION: An increase in extent or intensity.

"Better hold on tight; here comes the night."
—Little Big Town

November 3, 2000

Before the doctors could treat the cancer in Dad's pancreas, they had to tackle the jaundice, so they inserted a shunt to drain the bile.

Must I remember? My dad, once a strapping farm boy, who weighed more than three hundred pounds at his peak, was lying in a bed in a hospital in Columbus, Ohio, hooked up to tubes moving fluids that weren't supposed to be there from places I didn't want to know about. When he got up to use the bathroom, his robe parted in the back. (Why can't hospitals provide at least a measure of modesty to go with their two-dollar robes?) Instead of a strapping farm boy surging out of bed to conquer cancer, a pale, weak, tottering man gave up his dignity just to make it to the bathroom.

I knew then that I was to become the man of the family. I didn't desire that role. I was only thirty-one. I was supposed to have a little more time to mature properly. My boys needed a grandpa until their dad was ready; my wife needed me to hear Dad's advice; I needed to know him more so I could better know myself.

There, finally, I understood clearly: cancer had leveled a worthy father and elevated an unworthy son. Damn that cheap hospital robe. I'm not just swearing; it is a request: "Please, God, send sickness and death where they belong. One day, you will make all things right. Please, please, let it be today."

I managed not to cry until I exited his room. I had at least that much strength. Nobody in that wing of the hospital looked at me oddly when I exited his room and plodded down the hallway, crying openly.

Leaving the cold sterilization of impending doom, I stumbled out of the hospital and drove to Mom and Dad's house through the darkest of Columbus nights.

> I REMEMBER YOUR MOM AND DAD COMING TO OUR HOUSE ON A SUNDAY AFTERNOON TO LISTEN TO OUR PAIN. MY DAD HAD JUST DIED AT SIXTY-THREE, AND WE HAD JUST COME BACK TO OHIO FROM THE FUNERAL ... I MISS YOUR DAD.
> —SL

I remember sitting on hard, cool, wooden benches in church on sweltering summer Sunday mornings in Alabama, with my dad's arm slung casually over the back of the pew. He was (and still is, in my mind) bigger than life. Nothing could harm me under my dad's arm. Mom was comfort; Dad was strength. I even remember how disappointed I was when I was too big to sit on his lap anymore. I felt old, too big too fast.

I think of how my sons AJ and Braden and Vincent must feel now. Do I seem impenetrable, superheroish? When Vincent went to the ER for dehydration, did the needle in his hand fade away when he rested his head on Dad's broad shoulder? When I hug Braden at night, does he sleep better? When I go to AJ's basketball games, does my presence make a difference?

I put my arm around AJ last Sunday while Braden sat on my lap. They will need that memory some day. When I let Vincent sleep in our bed when he crawls in at two o'clock in the morning, or when I carry him around the entire Grand Rapids Zoo on my shoulders, I think it has more to do with me than it does with him.

Mom, Dad, Sonya and I

November 21, 2000

Dad's surgery took place on the longest day of my life. It was four days before Thanksgiving. I was desperately grateful for the friends and family in the lobby as we waited for news throughout the day, but I also wanted to be alone. They couldn't understand what I felt any more than I could understand what they felt.

How do I know what a wife of over thirty-five years feels? How do I know what goes through a brother's mind? A daughter's mind? A sister's? A friend's? We prayed and stayed, little clumps of grief huddled together, trying to make an island of hope in an ocean of surgical despair. Conversation was awkward and oddly shallow. I had two choices: talk about topics that were of no significance on that day, or talk about the fact that my dad was undergoing a long-shot surgery for a few extra years of life. Silence was lonely but preferred. The hours groaned past.

At one point, a doctor came out to the waiting room to somberly inform us that the surgery was going to be dicey, because some necessary stuff was wrapped around and pushing against the pancreas in some very unhelpful ways. You're in trouble when even the good things in your body work against you.

When we finally got a postsurgery update, the doctors told us it was "not a clean surgery," or something like that, which was a clinically detached but merciful way of saying that my father would inevitably die. Chemo and radiation might—might—prolong his life, but they would also lessen its quality. The doctor counseled against it, and we agreed.

I think that, deep inside, as we all forced weary smiles through tear-stained cheeks and headed back to my parents' home for supper, we all knew what was coming.

January 2001

Dad flew to a holistic medical and natural clinic in Germany for the first of two visits for cancer treatment. This world-renowned clinic offered a last-ditch effort to do what modern medicine could not. Reports were encouraging: the clinic had a great track record at prolonging life and its quality; Dad's digestive tract was recovering from the Whipple surgery; he had more energy; he could "stretch without pain." The staff loved his attempts to speak German with them. Because he grew up in Amish country in Pennsylvania, Dad knew a form of German (Pennsylvania Dutch), but that's not the same as real German. I'm sure the staff was entertained. Dad traveled to castles and forests and out-of-the way shops on his good days, writing home about the oddness of eating at a McDonald's in an old castle he toured.

Still, in spite of all the positive notes, five years of life for a pancreatic cancer patient is a miracle. Anything over two years is a gift. I prayed for a miracle, hoped for at least a gift, and planned for neither.

While he was in Germany, I turned thirty-two; AJ turned five. Dad turned fifty-five. He had two more years to go.

Dad was always proud of being big and strong. Not a bad kind of proud, but his strength meant something to him. More than once, when he was younger, he would put the back of his head on one chair and his heels on another and have people sit on his stomach while he stayed straight as a board. I remember his working in the field in a sleeveless T-shirt, which was pretty bold for a Mennonite farm boy, and equally embarrassing for his really cool son.

He seemed kind of old to be doing that (in my opinion), but he was probably only five or six years older than I am now. I still work on my tan during the summer, and I don't even have the grace to wear a T-shirt and spare the onlookers.

Funny how age changes perspective. I think he was bothered by his weight gain when he got older; I think accepting his gaunt frame was even tougher before he died. I know this because I am like my father, and it would bother me.

Summer 2001

When they visited my family in Traverse City again, in the postsurgery era, I remember pulling into my driveway as Mom and Dad finished a short walk. My sister had warned me that Dad did not look good. She was not even close. When I first saw him walking down the road toward my drive, literally half the man he once was, with Mom bravely holding his hand and smiling determinedly, I had to look away.

I hesitate to acknowledge that I scarcely looked at him again that weekend. Was I weak, or was the depth of my love was so great that I could not bear to see him? Yellow was a world away, and a pleasant world at that. Bring back the yellow Dad! I hugged him gingerly, desperately, afraid I would break him and terrified to let him go.

By this time, AJ was five and Braden was almost two. AJ was old enough to know something was not quite right; Grandpa walked slowly and gingerly. Braden did not understand. Still, the boys held back that first night, not sure how to interact with gaunt Grandpa. Eventually they ran and played with him, screeching and jumping on him as he sat in an overstuffed chair in our living room. I think it hurt and exhausted him to play with them, but he did anyway. Premonition, perhaps, from both sides. The boys had a ball, and Dad bravely soldiered on throughout the evening, as he did through the weekend.

Dare I say I was glad to see him leave? Not because I wanted him to go. God, no. The child in me wanted to cling to him. I wanted to jump on his lap too, like I did when I was young and he was bigger than life. Now, he was smaller than life, barely bigger than death, and I was no longer young. The child in me grieved my loss while my children celebrated his presence.

I wanted him to go because my life was shattering, and I was too weak to watch. (Foolish boy--how did I think I was going to get away from it?) Moses

> MY DEAR GRANDMA WOULD ALWAYS LET ME SIT ON HER LAP AND PUT HER ARM AROUND ME, NO MATTER HOW OLD I GOT, OR HOW OLD SHE GOT. EVEN AFTER I HAD CHILDREN, AND SHE WAS SO FRAIL I WAS AFRAID SHE'D BREAK, SHE'D TELL ME TO COME SIT ON HER LAP WHEN I CAME HOME TO VISIT. OH, HOW I WISH I COULD DO THAT AGAIN.
> —SM

had Aaron to hold up his arms; when my dad waved good-bye, from my house that weekend and from the world later, he lifted his arm without my help.

Once again, I had trouble looking him in the eye. I have trouble looking people in the eye to this day. I did not realize there is so much of chaos and the void under the eyebrows of the broken.

I did not see him again for another sixteen months. Distance is a cushion of sorts, though perhaps not a good one. Phone and e-mail updates are easier than visual ones, I think. My family experienced the hard work of proximity. I lived eight hours away, separated by geographical and emotional miles, and I was not there to help.

Dad reading a book.

Last visit: Ohio, in the coolness of the fall 2002. The cold of winter waited impatiently. The fall was taking too long.

During our visit that Thanksgiving, Dad and I drove to "our" Panera Bread on Broad Street in Columbus, Ohio. We both drank coffee, which sounds like an odd milestone to mark, but we had not done this in a while because of his diet. We ordered and then walked slowly down a side street and talked more intimately than we had in years.

I discovered that Dad had attended the same school where I was now taking master's classes. Apple and tree, I guess. We talked philosophy, and theology, and kids. Our time together was good, but we couldn't walk too long. He pushed himself; he tired easily. I was glad to see him up and moving, but when walking three blocks is death-defying, death is only three blocks away. We drove home, warm with coffee and camaraderie. My family drove back to Traverse City the next day.

> THE MEMORIES YOU HAVE SHARED MADE ME SMILE AND CRY, SOMETIMES SIMULTANEOUSLY. I TEND TO BURY MYSELF IN BOOKS WHEN THINGS GET TO BE TOO MUCH, AS THEY FREQUENTLY DID AT THAT TIME. I REALLY MISS DAD.
> —MY SISTER, SONYA

That was the last time I saw him alive.

Since that walk, I stop and buy coffee at Panera Bread as often as I can. It is my last connection with Dad. When I am in Panera, I can sense him just three blocks over. Out of the corner of my eye he is up, moving, strolling down Broad Street, gliding over late autumn leaves, enjoying a guilt-free cappuccino, finally free of the burden of outwalking death.

That was Thanksgiving. We did not go down to Columbus for Christmas. We had just been there, right? I suppose it accomplishes nothing to wonder what would be different today if I could go back and redo that holiday.

January 9, 2003

I think we got the phone call on a Thursday. Night.

I scrambled to find someone to coach my basketball team on Friday because Dad had "taken a turn for the worse," according to the initial phone call. Whoever called was trying to be gentle, but what a stupid euphemism. He hadn't gently veered off course. He hadn't mistakenly gone south instead of north. Whoever called me should have just told me he was dying. Then maybe I wouldn't have been at the store getting cat food, thinking that somehow my presence in Ohio was going to matter, when Sheila had to answer The Call.

When I walked through the sliding back door, my family stood frozen in the kitchen, immobilized and muted by grief and shock. My wife was crying by the counter, AJ sat soberly at the kitchen table, and Braden stood uncertainly by the sink. This scene is seared into my memory.

Is it good or bad that Braden did not understand? Sheila just looked at me with tears in her eyes and a haunted look I will never forget. If the eyes really are the windows to the soul, then when the soul does not know what to do, perhaps the eyes don't either.

There is an aching, an emptiness, a deep, haunting hollowness. Nothing prepares you. You can't practice grief. AJ, with all the depth of his seven years, said

> I REMEMBER EXACTLY WHERE I WAS AND WHAT I WAS DOING WHEN I HEARD THE NEWS ABOUT YOUR DAD .... I GUESS THE ONLY WAY TO AVOID THE GUT-WRENCHING PAIN OF LOSS IS, AS THE SAYING GOES, NEVER TO HAVE LOVED AT ALL. I THINK THE LOVE IS STILL WORTH THE TRADE-OFF.
> —LPS

very solemnly, "I think you know," and he said it with a voice that belied his youth. He hurdled years of adolescence in that moment. (Poor boy. Only four days before, we had come home from a birthday jaunt for him to hear a message on the machine from Mom and Dad. At least the last words of a grandfather to a grandson were good ones: "Happy birthday, AJ.")

We all hugged, but we had to get Braden to join our circle because his three and a half years had not prepared him to understand why we were crying or why we had to leave. What is death to a three-year-old? It was ten o'clock at night, and we had to get to Ohio NOW, as if that would help. We had to pack NOW, though I ended up buying new clothes for the funeral because nothing I owned was suitable for a funeral. I had to stay strong for at least eight hours yet.

> "Every hour wounds.
> The last one kills."
> — Neil Gaiman,
> American Gods

Every phone call I made I barely finished, but I communicated enough. Most people knew my dad had cancer, so when I started a sentence with "My dad …" and then had to stop because I was crying, people got it. It was one thing to call people and say Dad was sick. It was quite another to call them back and say the words, "Dad died. I have to leave so I can bury my father."

I am glad that, in all those phone calls that night, I pushed through and said he died. I needed to say it out loud. I did not use gentle euphemisms. He didn't "pass away," or "pass on," or "pass" or "fall asleep," or anything else, for that matter.

He turned yellow. He died.

There is no gentle way to explain either one.

I did not then, and I do not now.

"BUT PLEASE, PLEASE, WON'T YOU—CAN'T YOU GIVE ME SOMETHING THAT WILL CURE [FATHER]?"

UP TILL THEN HE HAD BEEN LOOKING AT THE LION'S GREAT FEET AND THE HUGE CLAWS ON THEM; NOW, IN HIS DESPAIR, HE LOOKED UP AT ITS FACE. WHAT HE SAW SURPRISED HIM AS MUCH AS ANYTHING IN HIS WHOLE LIFE. FOR THE TAWNY FACE WAS BENT DOWN NEAR HIS OWN AND (WONDER OF WONDERS) GREAT SHINING TEARS STOOD IN THE LION'S EYES. THEY WERE SUCH BIG, BRIGHT TEARS COMPARED WITH DIGORY'S OWN THAT FOR A MOMENT HE FELT AS IF THE LION MUST REALLY BE SORRIER ABOUT HIS [FATHER] THAN HE WAS HIMSELF.

"MY SON, MY SON," SAID ASLAN. "I KNOW. GRIEF IS GREAT."

—C. S. LEWIS, *THE MAGICIAN'S NEPHEW*

THE FUNERAL

FUNERAL: A ceremony marking a person's death; a ceremony to honor a deceased person.

"I do not want the peace the passeth understanding; I
want the understanding that bringeth peace."
—Helen Keller

"Do not seek death. Death will find you."
—Dag Hammarskjold

January 2003

In preparation for the funeral, I got a haircut and bought a new outfit. I don't know why. I looked at the clothes I packed and decided they did not do justice to the occasion. I bought black pants and a dark green shirt. The shirt still hangs in the closet next to one of my dad's shirts.

I also bought music: the New Gaither Vocal Band, southern gospel at its best (?). The style took me back to happier days in Alabama, to shuckin' corn, fried okra, fish fries, and the southern comfort of a childhood with a father. The lyrics sustained me on the drive down I-65.

> *"Oh come, angel band, come and around me stand. Oh, bear me away on your snowy wings to my immortal home."*
> *"Well, I'm on my way to heaven, and I'm so glad."*
> *"Satisfied? I'm satisfied. He said He would be my comfort; He said He would be my guide."*

For the record, I do not experience funerals as celebrations on this side of heaven. Even Jesus cried when his friend Lazarus died, and he rebuked the people for not weeping when funeral dirges played. Our emotions ought to match reality. Yes, Dad is in heaven. Good. "That's one home," Grandpa would say. But the grief of losing my dad makes me want to be in heaven too, not remain in this vale of tears and sorrow.

I have an idea: Can we not sing happy praise choruses for once? Let's not pretend something is happening here that is not. I am still on this fallen, miserable planet earth. Cancer invaded the pancreas of my father and killed him.

If Dad had been in the twilight of a good life, and it was clearly time for him to leave, I might have felt differently. But that's not what happened. I grieve for myself, thank you very much. I grieve for my mom, and my sisters, and for all the people who loved my father. I grieve for my boys, who have lost their innocence along with their grandfather. (At the viewing, Braden was sure Grandpa was sleeping, and poor, poor AJ tried to convince him that Grandpa was dead before I arrived to resolve the argument.) I grieve for all the people my dad could have counseled in the future. I grieve for my wife, who not only has to watch me go through this, but who will inevitably start thinking about this upcoming day in her future.

Don't tell me it is a celebration; don't tell me it will be okay; don't tell me this will pass. It's not okay. My father died. It won't pass, unless you are a Victor Frankenstein, planning on bringing him back. It will not pass. It is now part of my life. There is no transience here.

This—apologies to Gandalf—this *shall not pass*. I did not ask for the ring to be given to me. Nobody does, of course; nobody does. I had been given the ring of fatherlessness. And as much as I would like to destroy it and change what I had been given, and as grateful as I am for the companions who will walk with me, not even the fires of Mount Doom will melt my grief.

> MY HUSBAND SAID WORDS VERY SIMILAR TO YOU WHEN HE LOST HIS FATHER .... LIFE NEVER GETS BACK TO NORMAL, IT IS FOREVER CHANGED.
> —LR

People read short eulogies and poems at Dad's funeral, but I did not. When asked if I wanted to contribute, I declined. Others pulled together emotions and thoughts well enough to communicate how my dad's fifty-seven years of life impacted them. I could not. I asked the person in charge to simply say that my life would be my witness, my eulogy, to the man who was my father. That gives me decades in which to make a speech. (Was? Even now, must I always speak of him in the past?)

> *Dad stood up for what he believed. When I was a kid in Alabama, my parents attended Oak Drive Church, a new, racially integrated church at a time when integration was not popular. My parents were often followed as they drove to church, but that never stopped them.*
>
> *One weekend when I was in Bible college, some friends of mine stayed at my house overnight. We all crashed on the living room floor, surrounded by pillows and sleeping bags. Morning found my roommate and his girlfriend innocently snuggled up next to each other on the floor. When my dad strode out of the bedroom, he took one look, immediately woke them, and said, "Not in my house." It was awkward; I thought I would have to apologize for the stodgy old man, but my friend respected my dad for saying that.*

At the viewing in Columbus, AJ tried to explain to Braden that Grandpa was dead, not sleeping.

17

Sheila and I were in a side room with the Ohio friends and coworkers, sharing memories of Dad. I did not know anything was wrong until an agitated AJ came up to me. Apparently Braden kept insisting that Grandpa was sleeping; AJ could not convince him otherwise, so I explained to Braden that Grandpa would not wake up any more. I don't remember any details of that conversation, though I know it occurred. Honestly, I don't try. Why would I want to remember? Some moments in life, especially those surrounding death, are best left buried. God was merciful to me, it seems, though not so merciful to my eldest son.

For years, AJ could not bear to have us leave him for even the most ordinary reasons. He was not like that before Grandpa died. If hope is a thing with feathers, trust is a thing with wings, and when an eight-year-old has to convince his three-year-old brother that Grandpa is dead, a migration begins, and it is years before the rustle of wings returns. Migrations take awhile.

I, too, remember what it was like when hope and trust took flight, as if even they could not bear the coldness that had entered my father and then the world. They left silently, leisurely, the beating of their wings blending with and then giving place to the sound of red Alabama dirt hitting the casket of my father.

> LIFE IS FILLED WITH LOSSES ... LOSSES THAT CHANGE THINGS ... CHANGE US. I, TOO, FIND MYSELF THINKING ABOUT THE "UPCOMING DAY IN MY LIFE." I KNOW IT WILL COME, BUT I DON'T LOOK FORWARD TO IT.
> —ARS

But it was also in that moment, between the clink of the shovels and the thud of the clay and the sobs of my family, that I heard the incoming wings of a dove more clearly than ever before.

I withdrew into myself and stayed there a long time. During the drive from Michigan to Ohio, when I had to stay awake and strong for eight hours, I closed the relational part of myself down. I couldn't do it completely, but I think I instantly made a subconscious connection: Love in life is directly related to pain in death.

My instinctive response was not to love those around me harder, but to make myself impenetrable.

If nobody can get in, nobody has to eventually go.

I Hardened My Heart on a Thursday

I hardened my heart on a Thursday;
I had to drive south through the night.
Friday morning Mom's hug broke it open,
But since then it's been pretty tight.

I shut down my eyes on that Saturday,
The viewing did not need more tears.
That Sunday I shut them much tighter,
And now I've been squinting for years.

With a shovel, I buried my father that Monday,
On Tuesday, without one, I buried him more.
When on Wednesday we drove home,
Fleeing from Atmore,
I buried his memory deep in my core.

Now the drive to be healed is a chisel;
Father Time lends strength to each blow.
And I'm digging my way through my soul
To the core,
To liberate memories I need more and more.

*For more on Emotions, see page 88.

19

THE AFTERMATH: YEAR ONE

AFTERMATH: THE CONSEQUENCES OF AN EVENT (ESPECIALLY A CATASTROPHIC EVENT), ESPECIALLY AS RELATED TO AN INDIVIDUAL.

There are things that we don't want to happen but have to
accept; things we don't want to know but have to learn;
people we can't live without but have to let go.
—Author Unknown

I dreamed of my dad in the next months, vividly.

In my dreams we talked. We cried. We hugged. In ways I cannot explain, my dad visited me for months after his death.

This was one of the strangest parts in the entire saga. These dreams were not the "giant kangaroo chasing me through a field of marshmallows" dreams. These were dreams that broke down the barriers that normally separate real time from sleepy time.

I have had interesting experiences with dreams before. As an adult, I struggled for several years with serious nightmares. It finally got so bad, I had to learn how to manipulate my dreams. I now know this is called "lucid dreaming." When I learned how to do this, the nightmares stopped.

The dreams I had about my dad were neither bizarre nor terrifying. They were neither vague nor lucid. I could not manipulate them, or my dad would have stayed.

They started a couple of months after Dad died. "Dreams are from God," Joseph said, and now I know what he meant. My last conversation with Dad occurred during our trip to the Panera. (I'm still not sure if my distance spared me of grief or robbed me of love.) But sleep ushered me into a world I did not expect.

I would meet Dad in my dreams—sometimes with Mom, sometimes with other significant people in my life, sometimes by himself. We would talk, and I don't mean dream talk. We really had conversations. I poured out my questions and disillusionments and fears; he listened and offered advice and hope. I asked him why he died; I asked him why I should pray; I asked what to do with my grief.

I asked him why he had to go.

I don't remember all the details; I just know he walked with me, and he talked with me, and he told me everything would be okay. I would hug him when our time was up, and I hated every good-bye. He always walked off into a distance that was murky to me and beautiful to him. He

> I FEAR THE DAY I LOSE
> THE MOST IMPORTANT
> MEN IN MY LIFE AND
> I PRESENTLY GRIEVE
> THE LOSS OF ONE WHO
> WENT TOO SOON.
> —KG

loved talking to me, but he couldn't wait to go back home. At least four times I had these dreams; on at least four occasions I spent time with my father after he died.

This was not one-second REM brain static. I would wake up crying, my pillow soaked, my heart melted, my body trembling.

I believed then, and I believe now, that God allowed my dad visitation rights to help bring closure to a son who never had a chance to say good-bye. I was not there when he had to wade through the waters, but I was there four times while God troubled them.

Many people would tell me that my brain was just firing neurons that sparked neutrinos that created a phantasm out of my memories that looked a lot like my dad, and I talked to … myself … four times.

They are wrong. Joseph said dreams are from God, and for four times over the span of a year, my dad arrived courtesy of the Dream Maker.

I knew each time, lying in bed, listening to the whispers of his voice fade, that everything would be okay.

> GOD WALKS THROUGH EVERY PART OF OUR LIVES. JUST AS WE WALK IN HIS WORLD, HE'S SO EVER PRESENT IN OURS. I KNOW HE VISITS AND FASHIONS OUR DREAMS.
> —ARS

---

*For more on <u>Dreams</u>, see page 92.

Dad was childlike all his life. (Not childish—there's a big difference.) He loved to imitate people. (His Jerry Clower imitation amused him and occasionally others for years: "There was five forks sticking in the back of Uncle Versey's hand!") As a teacher at a Bible college that attracted students from all over the world, he met students from many nations. He gleefully attempted multiple foreign dialects with varying amounts of success, much to the dismay (and secret amusement) of his really cool teenage children.

When we "truck farmed," raising day lilies, peppers, raspberries, and cherry tomatoes, he constantly photographed the same lilies and talked about them excitedly to everyone who would listen. He drove his mini-tractor around as if it were one of the real tractors he drove as a young man, and when he bought a bigger tractor one year, well, that was a good year. He told everyone about the French chef who used our lilies to garnish salads in a Columbus bistro; I often heard the story of how Dad's raspberries provided dessert for Geraldine Ferraro when she visited the governor's mansion.

Dad would buy Coke in a McDonald's drive-through window with the pleasure of a kid, then explain it to Mom by saying he was, and I quote, "worried he would get dehydrated" in the fifteen minutes it took to get home. I still smile at that one.

Dad with his two brothers, Phil and Jim.

For about three months after Dad died, I dragged myself to school day after day; one day, through my tears, I asked a close friend, who understood death: "Is it okay that I don't want to live anymore?"

> "I could swear I have two hearts, one to stay, one to depart."
> —Downhere

He understood what I meant. I didn't mean I wanted to commit suicide; I didn't mean that the rest of my life would be some type of living hell to which death was preferable. I meant that the ache in my heart felt so big that only an eternity with Dad could fill it.

So, I asked my friend if what I felt was okay, and he said it was. Someone once said that grief is the price we pay for love, and when the love is deep, so is the grief. Ah, then, now I know. My love was deep.

Life passes by in a fog. No one tells you that the funeral lingers. In fact, no one tells you a lot of things.

No one tells you that viewing is something you will dread but still cherish.

No one tells you that people make so many shallow but well-intentioned comments.

No one tells you that the viewing is the last place you want to be, but it's also the only place you want to be.

No one tells you that a casket with a dead father sears your soul.

No one tells you how horrifying it is to decide whether or not to touch him, or kiss him, or maybe even just look at him while he is in the casket.

No one tells you how important—and how inadequate—eulogies are.

> READING THAT MADE ME THINK OF THE DAYS LEADING UP TO THE VIEWING AND FUNERAL OF MY DAD, AND THE ACTUAL DAYS OF BOTH .... THANK YOUR FOR WRITING IT DOWN AND SHARING BECAUSE IN MY CASE IT MADE ME FEEL LIKE IT ISN'T JUST ME.
> —KA

No one tells you that you want to bury him, because this experience is hell, but when the lid finally closes and the ropes begin to lower him, your grief is a bottomless well.

No one tells you that the funeral is the easy part.

No one tells you that the loneliest nights are not the ones preceding the funeral, when friends and family are near, and when adrenaline is still raging. It's not even the night of the funeral. No, the nights that crush you are one week, five weeks, three months later, while sitting on your back deck at night, family in bed, the reality of your loss pressing you into the cushions of your chair while you offer up prayers for solace that you secretly fear are as ineffectual as the ones that failed to save a man much better than you.

No one tells you that, while meandering through an ordinary day, doing ordinary things— say, you are driving—you will suddenly be *there,* with your dad, and you will be crushed for thirty seconds by the weight of that memory. You will have to pull over until the grief lets up enough so you can ease back into the traffic, and then you re-enter the flow of life, just a little more broken than before.

That is what no one tells you.

> "YOU WERE CRUSHED FOR THIRTY SECONDS" … IS SOMETHING I EXPERIENCED JUST THIS MORNING THINKING ABOUT THE END OF MY MARRIAGE …. EVERY NOW AND THEN, REMEMBERING THE GOOD THINGS OF THE MOMENT ARE LOST IN THE WASH OF PAIN FROM YESTERDAY.
> —OM

Dad had too big a heart, yet he was intimidating to people. He was a big man, sometimes gruff and outspoken. I treasure the image of him walking down a hallway at the Bible college, professorial brow furrowed, eyes piercing. In spite of his appearance, he was a teddy bear inside. He worked in a prison as a chaplain's assistant for years, and I think the countless stories of broken and trampled lives brought out a tenderness (and perhaps a weariness) in him that would not have been there otherwise. Lifers tell stories that will keep you awake at night.

My grandpa, the prison chaplain and one of the most godly men I know, collected homemade knives the prisoners turned in to him. I think my dad must have collected stories.

While he worked at the prison in Alabama, my parents ran a home for delinquent girls. In Ohio, Dad counseled people, and he and Mom remained friends with his clients for years, giving them time and energy and money and going out of their way to visit them on trips and follow their lives. We took into our home people who desperately needed love and family. I don't know if professionals recommended this approach, but it's what we did. It is who he was.

When a windstorm swept through Traverse City last October, the winds blew so strongly that a poplar tree next to our house broke. At least, I think it did. I was standing on the back deck, embracing the storm, when I heard the tree "pop." It was deep; it wasn't a "crack" like a branch or a twig makes. I kind of expected the tree to fall, but it didn't. In fact, to this day it still stands there, sprouting happy green leaves every spring, and carrying on as if nothing happened.

But I know.

I know that, in the midst of one particular storm, something broke deep inside that tree, and it will never be the same again. Even though that tree still looks good, something is not right inside, and never will be again.

This I know.

Dad teaching

July 2003

About six months after Dad's funeral, we drove to a family reunion in Tennessee. AJ had changed since the fateful night he waited in the kitchen with his mother and brother, thinking that we were going to Ohio because Grandpa had taken a "turn for the worse." He was the one who told me, as his innocence leaked out with his tears, "I think you know." Even today, my heart aches for my son.

Is it any wonder he had changed? He understood what it meant that Grandpa had died. That must be hard for a child to process. Unfortunately, I was not engaged with him in the aftermath of the funeral.

Here's the irony: I so missed my father that I pulled back from my sons. I let Sheila raise AJ and Braden. I wasn't trying to be manipulative; I wasn't trying to get sympathy; I didn't want to be like that. I just couldn't do it. Day after day, I did not have it in me to be a father.

One afternoon while we were in Tennessee, six of my male cousins and I were sitting in an outdoor hot tub in the middle of the day—odd memory, that one—while AJ ran boldly where no eight-year-old should have run, making more noise than even a eight-year-old should have made. I sat in the hot tub watching Sheila chase him down, and I mumbled some sort of half-hearted explanation along the lines of, "I just haven't felt like parenting lately," as if everyone would understand. But they had not lost their fathers; they did not understand.

THE AFTERMATH: YEAR TWO

About suffering they were never wrong, the old Masters:
how well they understood its human position:
how it takes place while someone else is eating,
or opening a window, or just walking dully along.

—W. H. Auden, *Musee des Beaux Arts*

January 2004

Here I am, two years later, and I can tear up on a moment's notice. Quick images, passing thoughts: they come out of nowhere, making the world hazy and leaving me slightly unsteady. Those fleeting thoughts get me, true, but the slow thoughts are the worst.

"I have no father," I finally said the other day. I didn't want to say it, as if somehow not saying it would mean his death wasn't real, like some verbal equivalent to the "monster under the bed" scenario of my youth. A running start and a leap in the dark used to keep me clear of the clutches of some hidden and horrible monstrosity. Maybe some verbal (or nonverbal) gymnastics could have the same effect inside me now. Unfortunately, I run more slowly than I used to, and the night is darker in more serious ways, and the monsters have much longer arms.

I can't think about his absence much, or I realize how alone I feel in this world. No offense to my wife, or my kids, or my friends, but I have no dad to do what good dads do: affirm my decisions; take pride in what I have become; give me advice; hug me with a manly hug.

I miss the big, enveloping hug of a father. His last two years did not allow for that kind of hug, but the ones he mustered still seemed like that in my head. What men in my life will fill that role? Is this where God steps in and becomes more obvious? I think He already has, and maybe He will even more. I am counting on that.

No offense, God, but I miss my dad's rough, unshaven chin, and the smell of Brut, and the old-school flannel shirt, and the tenderness and awkwardness of the man hug.

That is what I cannot regain.

> In several days, I will have been motherless for six months. The fog and haze cause much uncertainty in me .... even though I may be a novice at grief, one thing I am certain of: my life is forever changed.
> — BA

GERTRUDE: "WHY DO THE CLOUDS SEEM TO HANG ON YOU?"

HAMLET: "SEEM? NAY, NOT SEEM, MOTHER. IS ... I HAVE THAT WITHIN ME THAT PASSETH SHOW. THESE ARE BUT THE TRAPPINGS AND THE SUITS OF WOE."

—SHAKESPEARE, HAMLET, ACT I, SCENE 2

April 2004

It's funny: I miss things now about my dad that I didn't think mattered that much when I was young and foolish. I now treasure memories that seemed insignificant when he was alive. Driving to the end of our half-mile driveway to wait for the bus in a humiliatingly old, puke green pick-up truck; playing Stratego and chess with me for an evening by the wood stove; listening to Garrison Keillor on wintry Saturday nights; working in the day lilies and peppers and raspberries; furtively watching *60 Minutes* and the Olympics on our contraband Mennonite TV; working hard in the field and knowing he was proud of me; going to work with him in Alabama when he was putting down vinyl floors; listening to his old friends reminisce about him; watching him entertain international students at our home as we cooked meals with mysterious ingredients and tried to pronounce words with even more mysterious nuances; hearing the same joke for the thirtieth time and still finding it kind of funny; talking theology as I explained all the things about God that he should know, followed by him casually reminding me that he had read my "new" book years ago.

He told Mom in his final years that he enjoyed talking with me as one adult to another. I don't think he could have said anything more meaningful to me.

WHEN I WAS AT ROSEDALE. I REMEMBER ... WALKING INTO THE OTHERWISE DARK AND QUIET CHAPEL TO HEAR LEON PLAYING MOZART AT THE PIANO IN THE DARK. ALWAYS THE SAME PIECE, BUT I LOVED IT .... I WANTED TO BE ABLE TO DO THAT LATER IN LIFE. I WOULD LISTEN FOR A WHILE BEFORE I LEFT, RELISHING THE FEELING, IMAGINING I UNDERSTOOD THE ROLE OF MUSIC TO CALM, FOCUS, TRANSPORT SOMEONE SO BUSY AND PULLED IN SO MANY DIRECTIONS. THAT IS HOW I WILL ALWAYS REMEMBER YOUR DAD, AND THE MEMORY IS SWEET.
—OM

Perspective is important.

My flesh believed that his passing was a tragedy, but it wasn't tragic for him, just for those of us left behind.

My flesh believed I would not get over it, but I am. Death is part of life, and I should have expected that He who conquered and holds the key to death would pass that victory along to His children somehow. Neither the dead nor the living need fear the power of death anymore.

My flesh believed I would never forget, but I am. For the first couple of years, I could conjure a memory so vivid, so sweet, so real, that my eyes would always betray my will. Now I seem to have lost the ability to recapture that experience. This feels bad, but I wonder. Aren't we meant to move on? Are pictures perhaps a curse that keep the ever receding past too close? I cannot bring him back; what should I do? Watch videos in which his ghost struts on a stage that is no longer his to command? Why not focus on what he gained? His reward is found in neither his past nor mine.

My flesh and my spirit wish this world were mercifully short, but my time is not mine to decide. I must stand on the shoulders of giants like my father and, forgetting what lies behind, press on. "Further up and further in," Aslan calls, and I listen.

Some day my sons will live what I am living.

May they be able to remember the past without getting mired in it.
May they be able to live the present without forgetting the past.
May they be able to always find the glory that the future promises.

October 2004

I have no more dreams (is that also a gift?), and my memory of Dad is becoming frayed. "My father died not two weeks ago," said Hamlet, and Ophelia reminds him it was twice two months. "So long?" Hamlet replies, and now I know the feeling. We all know that memory fades, but that reality doesn't really sink home until we start to forget things that should never fade.

On the other hand, I don't like pictures and videos. A part of me thinks that perhaps some things are meant to be forgotten. He no longer lives; pictures seem to tell a lie. He is on my wedding video, walking and laughing and shaking hands. Must a reminder of laughter and life and love also be a reminder of death and passing? Perhaps I do not want to relive us except in my mind, in my memories, even though they fade. Is it wise to make a timeless image of something that is not timeless? I wonder. Perhaps some things were meant to fade. Most people don't understand.

But now …now … my mortality has begun to haunt about my doors. "I am too much in the sun," and I feel the burn. My dad's life was a candle, too brief; how long will mine burn? Braden snuggles into me on Sunday mornings, and I remember the warmth and strength and security that Dad's presence brought. When will they have to cross the same deep river that threatens to drown me? AJ cannot bear to be out of my sight; how long will this last? What will he do on the inevitable day when I am gone? Vincent knows I will hold him at first whimper; what will he do, my darling son, when one day he whimpers for me, and I cannot hold him?

My father died feeling that the end of his life had been wasted in spite of all the things he did in light of eternity. Perhaps Emily Dickinson had my father in mind—death was kind when it stopped for him.

I wonder if, in its kindness, my mind will stop my memories or preserve them.

I'm listening to E. V. Hill preach a sermon he delivered at the funeral of his wife. I need to hear the reminder that God, not Satan, holds the keys to death, hell, and the grave. I need to hear that Satan has to have permission to touch God's children. Life is not in the hand of Satan. I need to hear that eye has not seen and ear has not heard what God has prepared for those who love him.

I must remember.

Flesh and blood cannot inherit the kingdom of God.

I must remember.

The Lord gives and takes away. Oh, bless his name.

I must remember.

The corruptible must be shed to put on the incorruptible.

I must remember.

God will someday judge certain things in this world to have been false and damnable, a tragic twisting of how God intended the world to be. Death will be damned. It *will* be swallowed up in victory.

I must remember.

> IT BRINGS ME GREAT JOY THAT THEIR EARTHLY DESTINY DOES NOT END WITH THEIR LAST BREATH HERE .... IT'S LIKE THE DAYS I CATCH A GLIMPSE OF MY MOTHER IN THE MIRROR, OR AM REMINDED OF A HYMN SHE LOVED AND FIND MYSELF HUMMING ALONG. IT'S THOSE DAYS THAT I DON'T FEEL AS MUCH LIKE I'M CARRYING THE BATON ... I AM THE BATON.
> —GB

*For more thoughts on <u>Memory</u>, go to page 96.

IT SEEMED TO HIM THAT HE HAD STEPPED THROUGH A HIGH WINDOW THAT LOOKED ON A VANISHED WORLD. A LIGHT WAS UPON IT FOR WHICH HIS LANGUAGE HAD NO NAME. ALL THAT HE SAW WAS SHAPELY, BUT THE SHAPES SEEMED AT ONCE CLEAR CUT, AS IF THEY HAD BEEN FIRST CONCEIVED AND DRAWN AT THE UNCOVERING OF HIS EYES, AND ANCIENT AS IF THEY HAD ENDURED FOR EVER.

HE SAW NO COLOR BUT THOSE HE KNEW, GOLD AND WHITE AND BLUE AND GREEN, BUT THEY WERE FRESH AND POIGNANT, AS IF HE HAD AT THAT MOMENT FIRST PERCEIVED THEM AND MADE NAMES FOR THEM NEW AND WONDERFUL.

IN WINTER HERE NO HEART COULD MOURN FOR SUMMER OR FOR SPRING.

NO BLEMISH OR SICKNESS OR DEFORMITY COULD BE SEEN IN ANYTHING THAT GREW UPON THE EARTH.

ON THE LAND OF LORIEN THERE WAS NO STAIN.

—J. R. R. TOLKIEN

THE AFTERMATH: YEAR THREE

Because God is never cruel, there is a reason for all things. We must know the pain of loss; because if we never knew it, we would have no compassion for others, and we would become monsters of self-regard, creatures of unalloyed self-interest. The terrible pain of loss teaches humility to our prideful kind, has the power to soften uncaring hearts, to make a better person of a good one.

—Dean Koontz, *The Darkest Evening of the Year*

January 2005

Three years ago, I was driving to Ohio through the night with two sleeping boys: one digesting death from his seven years of life experience; one sleeping, too young to know anything but that he was going to see Grandma and Grandpa—well, not Grandpa (we haven't explained that yet). Sheila was trying to stay awake with me for eight lonesome hours. I had to get to Ohio, even though time was no longer of the essence.

We arrived in downtown Columbus at five o'clock in the morning. When Mom met us at the front door, calm and composed, everything still seemed unreal. The reality of why I was there didn't sink in until six o'clock, lying in my bed, across the hall from where my dad should have been sleeping. Sheila held me as my body finally, quietly, racked with sobs. I had to show restraint even then, because my kids were sleeping out their exhaustion on the floor right next to me, unaware of how everything had changed.

Now, three years later, I am ashamed that I forgot the anniversary of my father's death. I think about Dad all year long—he haunts my days—and then I forget the one day in which he should be remembered. Maybe remembered is not the best word, since I remember him constantly.

> He just stopped being there, but the world carried on anyway. It should have changed, just a little bit.
> —Lee Child, *Without Fail*

"Commemorate" is more appropriate. I forgot to commemorate until Mom and Sonya called me from beside his grave. Is it possible that such a good man can so easily slip from his only son's mind? Is that the way it is supposed to be?

April 2005

I realized recently that I don't fear death like I used to. Don't get me wrong: I'm not saying I think it will be pleasant at all. I just realized that somehow in the process of watching Dad's journey, death became far more tangible, more understandable. It's no longer the devil I don't know. I fear leaving my family to deal with the fallout, but that's probably not really fear. I guess it's more like grief: I grieve already for those others around me who will have to cope with my death some day. I already grieve for my boys.

As for me, I'm ready to go. I don't want my boys to mourn as I have mourned, but they will, at least in some fashion. I don't want my wife to be alone—my mom had some hard years—but if I go first, she will be a widow too. I know it is a common hardship in life, but that doesn't make it any easier. I already grieve for my wife.

That's why I don't want to leave.

But I am exhausted most days; when I make it home, I will finally relax. I don't feel like losing more people I love; "better to have loved than lost" is a poetic way of saying that love and loss are intertwined, and the greater the love, the more the separation undoes you for a time. I'm running the race, but I can get so caught up in putting one foot in front of the other that I forget the race isn't the point; the finish line is. As I'm writing this, I am listening to Mercy Me sing about heaven:

> *I'm gonna wrap my arms around my daddy's*
> *neck, and tell him that I missed him;*
> *and tell him all about the man that I became, and hope that it pleased him;*
> *there's so much I want to say, there's so much I want you to know,*
> *when I finally make it home.*

Now I'm crying again. Heaven? I am ready.

Spring Break, 2005
In Columbus, Ohio, before Mom moved to Alabama

THE LAST GARAGE SALE

Life will never be the same, I know
in my head but shield my heart.
People paw through our lives, paying 58 cents
for 58 years' worth of stuff in a cart.
My dad died fast; my mom's been slow
to leave her home, but wise.

In with the new, Life Part Two,
relentless and cold and kind.
I can't push it away, I don't really want to,
since a life and a house both have dust-laden stories,
memories that are now harder to find.

And as I drive away, garage empty, house bare, Mom receding,
once beautiful bridges burn their silhouette into my rearview mirror.

Mom is already building new southern bridges out of the ashes,
surrounded by okra, sweet tea, grandchildren, and red dirt.

My old bridges are
increasingly dim [and]
too easily forgotten [and]
precious beyond words [and]
Crumbling.

But new bridges emerge from the rubble;
snow-covered, spanning Great Lakes, populated by trolls,
built by the laughter of three children.

I have become a builder of beautiful bridges
That will one day also burn.

May the fire be warm, and full of light.

"ANTHONY, I REMEMBER EXACTLY WHERE I WAS WHEN I SAID,
'GOD, IT'S OKAY THAT YOU TOOK HIM.' UNANSWERED PRAYER?
SOMETIMES WE HAVE TO LEAVE THINGS ON THE SHELF AND KNOW
THAT OUR UNDERSTANDING IS FLAWED, BUT HIS IS PERFECT."
—MY MOM

"IT REALLY IS LIKE SEEING THROUGH A DARK, CLOUDED GLASS ...
BUT OUR LOVED ONES NOW CAN SEE IT CLEARLY FROM THE
OTHER SIDE. KIND OF MAKES ME ACHE TO BE THERE TOO."
—BBG

THE AFTERMATH: YEAR FOUR

It is not as a child that I believe and confess Jesus Christ.
My hosanna is born of a furnace of doubt.

—Dostoevsky

April 2006

I am reading the *Journal of the Death of a Good Man,* and I am crying again. It looks like I don't have to worry about the "not weeping." I wish I wouldn't cry—I can't wait until I don't—but I dread that day, too. At some point, I will be relieved of his memory and robbed of his life at the same time. I now understand what "bittersweet" means. Jesus said, "Blessed are those who mourn," and his wisdom has taken on new meaning. When the day comes that I do not mourn, I will not feel as blessed as I do now. I had a dad who was easy to love when he lived; a dad who made my heart ache when he left; a dad whose memory reminds me still that I have lived a blessed life rich with love, and laughter, and hope. I have a new prayer:

> Lord, if you will grant me one request, may it be that I always
> cry when I remember my father. If you grant a second request,
> may it be that there comes a day in this life that I don't.

When I was about thirteen, our family drove to Pennsylvania to visit relatives, and we stayed with Uncle Roy and Aunt Anna Mary. We went to one of the stores my uncle helped to oversee, and among other things I helped them carry several flats of raspberries. I carried too many, and I dropped eight quarts, which is like ten gallons in raspberry volume. All Dad said was, "Maybe don't carry so much next time."

When I was about sixteen, we bought a green mini-tractor, and I went tearing through newly plowed dirt with it, whipping the wheel back and forth to skid around. Dad just watched until I pulled the tractor back up to the house, then said ... I don't remember. It doesn't matter. He was kind of mad, but he understood my youthful nature.

When I was about seventeen, I drove our pick-up into a ditch and I didn't tell him. About a week later he said, "Do you know why the pick-up pulls to the left?" I did, and through many tears I told him. He said, "Why didn't you tell me?" And that was pretty much the end of it.

September 2006

The Bible records that Jacob wrestled with God while camping in the wilderness between Beersheba and Dan. Jacob was sleeping on the ground, using a rock for a pillow, when he awoke to discover an apparent foe. They wrestled the entire night. When the struggle ended, Jacob said two key things: "I will not let you go until you bless me," and, "Surely God was in this place, and I did not know it." As a result of this wrestling match, Jacob limped the rest of his life, but he was a changed man in other ways.

No one wants his father to die of pancreatic cancer in his fifties, but mine did. That's called a wilderness experience. Somewhere between Beersheba and Dan, I laid my father in the ground. For a time, I laid my head down upon a rock. When I awoke, I wrestled with God.

I still do. Sometimes I struggle half-heartedly, because He convinced me long ago that His grace is stronger than my doubt, but some days I fight with teeth bared and muscles aching. I do not let Him go. We have wrestled, He and I, and yet He has blessed me.

> I AM NOT AFRAID TO "WRESTLE" WITH GOD. I HAVE FOUND HIM TO BE MOST WILLING TO HEAR THE HEARTFELT GUT-WRENCHING STRUGGLES OF HIS MOST FINITE CREATURES. IN DOING SO, I ENJOY A DEEP SENSE THAT THERE IS NOTHING I CANNOT BRING TO HIM.
> —KJ

When AJ was eleven, he asked me, "Dad, how old are people when they struggle with what they believe?" ("Older than you, son. Go to sleep.")

Actually, I told him everybody in the world questions what they believe at some point. It's okay. Truth will win in the end, if you truly seek it. Everyone has times when the best pillows are rocks, and the most meaningful relationships are the ones in which we wrestle.

But if we don't let go, God will bless us.

GOD DOES NOT ALWAYS SAY "YES" NO MATTER HOW GOOD I THINK THE CAUSE IS. THIS, AT TIMES, HAS BROUGHT ABOUT A "CRISIS OF FAITH" WHERE A SITUATION NECESSITATES THAT I RECONCILE BETWEEN GOD BEING WRONG AND ME BEING WRONG. SINCE I KNOW IT'S NOT HIM, I MUST ASK HIM TO GIVE ME A NEW PERSPECTIVE. I HAVE STRUGGLED WITH THIS …. GOD HAS FAITHFULLY CHANGED MY PERSPECTIVE.

—PR

*For more musings on <u>Faith,</u> go to page 99.

December 2006

Our family flew to Atmore for Christmas, our first in the South with Dad's family since his death.

The flight there did not help. Vincent screamed for the maximal amount of time allotted to him, mostly while we were sitting on the tarmac waiting for our delayed plane to take off, warding off the escalating wrath of the commuters and the snippy questions from the stewardesses. After an eternity, we arrived in Pensacola and unloaded all our luggage—and baggage—into my sister's van.

It was the first major Weber family Christmas without Dad. It was my first return visit to his grave.

I delayed walking to the graveside for a couple of days, until I mustered my courage and drove to visit the dead.

In some ways, it felt like the funeral again. I didn't want to be there, but I had to be there as well. I wanted to be hard and unemotional like big boys are, but I couldn't. I wanted to pretend that I had somehow misunderstood reality, but words chiseled into a slab of granite are permanent.

> I WONDER ABOUT SO MANY THINGS IN REGARDS TO THE LOVE OF GOD AS WE SUFFER HERE IN THIS LIFE. PEOPLE SAY HE WALKS WITH US WHEN WE HURT. BUT I DON'T KNOW HOW YOU TELL …. UNLESS I GO PURELY ON FAITH. I WONDER IF THAT IS RIGHT.
> —KLM

Catharsis comes in many ways. A river of sorrow doesn't always drown us, I have discovered. Sometimes, our own tears water a dry and thirsty land, and that Christmas I spent some time in a lonesome graveyard, floating downstream, headed for a more beautiful country.

ALL THAT LINGERS IS NOT GOLD

All that lingers is not gold
Some of it is dross.
Much that I now carry in me
Should be at the cross.

Baggage that I calmly packed
I should have left behind, but
when it's time for baggage claim,
I always get in line.

An awful lot gets buried when
We throw the dirt down slow.
An awful lot of coffins hold
More dirt than we all know.

But gold comes through the fire pure,
And baggage sometimes goes;
And dirt can be the ground from which
A flower grows.

THE AFTERMATH: YEAR FIVE

Time goes, you say? Ah no! Alas, Time stays, *we* go.
—Henry Austin Dobson

March 2007

Time moves on. As I update this journal, I can read and not weep. Is that progress? Time truly stops for no man, not even those most deserving of at least a pause. I am distracted by the urgent and the present at the expense of the important and the past. I think more about my fluctuating weight than I do about my father. I watch the news and think it is a shame that people know more about a B-list actress who overdosed than they do of people like my dad.

I am disheartened by how quickly Dad's life fades from me. How can four short years of absence make his thirty-four years of presence with me seem so distant? Is this what will happen to my legacy when I die? Are we supposed to go so gently into the night, or is it my fault that I do not rage more?

I am gaining an appreciation for the epics I used to teach at school, where the classical heroes desperately fought to immortalize their names and exploits in the songs of the bards. Remembrance equaled immortality. Beowulf feels closer.

I used to read the stories and think that the heroes had their priorities all out of line (and maybe they did), but I get it now, and it adds to my grief. I feel like Dad's life is more *Ozymandias* than Beowulf.

> *And on the pedestal these words appear:*
> *"My name is Ozymandias, king of kings: Look*
> *on my works, ye Mighty, and despair!"*
> *Nothing beside remains.*
> *Round the decay*
> *Of that colossal wreck, boundless and bare. The*
> *lone and level sands stretch far away.*
> —Percy Bysshe Shelley, *Ozymandias*

Speaking of heroes, I am using *Smallville* to study heroes in youth group (the old-school superheroes, not the Watchmen). These people are brave, and pure, and strong, and committed to truth, and worthy of emulation. On good days, when I bask in my memories, I think my dad embodied all those things. On normal days, I know he didn't. He was human, not superhuman.

I still love him anyway, and miss him.

I was fat in Oregon. Well, I became fat. As an adult, I thought I was always a fat kid until I looked at pictures of me when I was younger. I wasn't fat until I moved to Oregon. The timeline of pudginess is irrelevant, I suppose. I just remember growing to be fat and learning to be lonely.

One birthday, it must have been my ninth, Dad took me to a pizza place, some kind of Chucky Cheese gig in Albany, Oregon, and I ate a whole small pizza by myself. I don't remember Mom or Dad ever saying anything to me about my weight. They might have, but I don't remember. I do remember that on my birthday, Dad let me eat a whole pizza by myself and didn't say a word. Thank you.

Dad, Grandma, and Uncle Phil

Someone unaware of how seasons work planned a family reunion in Georgia in the middle of July, so we drove from the balmy 75 degrees of Traverse City to the 95 degree humidity of Georgia for a family reunion.

This might sound really self-serving and narcissistic, but it's how I felt, and I am trying so hard to write honestly, so here we go.

As far as I know, my sister and I were the only cousins whose father had died, and my mom was the only widow there. Except for conversations between me, my sister and my mom, no one asked us how we were doing until the last day. No one.

In fact, no one would really talk about my dad. When we finally trotted out old family photos for a slide show Saturday afternoon (or "Mennonite movies," as I like to call them), pictures of my dad popped up, but no one made a comment to suggest anything was amiss. *("Hey, where is that big guy? I haven't seen him in, oh, about three years or so!")*

On the last day we took family pictures. That had been an emotional disaster two years before, and if we had been rearranging deck chairs for the previous two days, this time the *Titanic* was clearly going down. Everyone gathered in a variety of Weber clumpings *("Birthdays in January, over here on the hay bales now! And shiver like it's the right month!")* And still, through an entire photo shoot with fathered family after fathered family lining up, no one said a word to the one fatherless clump.

> ONE OF MY MEMORIES OF YOUR DAD IS HIM DRIVING IN OUR LANE ON THE RED MASSEY TRACTOR, BOUNCING ON THE SEAT AS HE HIT THE BUMPS AT THE END OF THE LANE. OFTEN HE WOULD STOP THE TRACTOR AND WITH A GENTLE BELLY LAUGH TELL SOME HUMOROUS STORY. AND I'LL NEVER FORGET THE SATURDAY MORNING HE STORMED INTO OUR HOUSE TELLING US TO TURN ON NPR AND WE ALL LAUGHED UNTIL WE CRIED—THAT WAS THE DAY I MET THE CLICK AND CLACK BROTHERS.
> —MI

Afterward, I saw Mom talking to my uncle Phil, my dad's youngest brother, who had finally breached the walls of memory, and the dam holding back Mom's grief and tears crumbled. I joined them under that white gazebo in Georgia, not because I was invited, but because I wanted to be a part of something, anything, that commemorated my father.

I just wanted someone to say, "I miss your dad." They didn't need to say anything else. I didn't need an opportunity to eulogize—I had passed that up once, and nothing had changed. All I would have needed to say was, "Me, too," and that would have been sufficient.

I just wanted to know that gone was not the same as forgotten.

But grief is a funny thing, and I know now that they were all grieving in their own way. They probably did not want to ruin my weekend; silence can be an act of love and care, too.

One of my uncles, Jim, Dad's other brother, kept going out of his way to talk to me all weekend. He was the second-born son, and I think he missed his older brother and didn't know what to do, so he talked to his brother's son.

I get it now.

Thanks, Uncle Jim. Thanks, Uncle Phil. Thank you to a family who quietly loved us and silently grieved with us. It is not your fault that my perspective on grief and loss was so distorted by me.

Dad's favorite dessert.

*For more on <u>Community</u>, see page 102.

THE AFTERMATH: YEAR SIX

When I awoke this morning, exhausted from my rest, a
demon dark and terrible was sitting on my chest.

—Steve Biddulph, *Manhood*

January 2008

When we lived in Oregon, we raised ducks and chickens and goats and lived on a farm where I shot bumblebees (legally) and doves (illegally) with my BB gun. The doves tasted disappointingly like chicken.

Dad and I trekked to the swift, cold Oregon rivers to collect agates and jasper, which we would polish in our neighbor's rock tumbler. I walked tea and hops fields with him in the summer as he moved huge irrigation towers and gathered soil samples. Summer jobs are crucial when working in Christian education. I know that now.

He spoke at youth camps, tolerated local Jesus Freak bands, and took vanloads of rowdy teens to tube and ski on Mount Hood, and I sometimes got to go along. He organized family movie nights at our traditional Mennonite church (Q: Who wants to see *Son of Flubber* and *The Computer Wore Tennis Shoes* on an old school projector? A: Mennonites.)

Does what he did then explain what I do now? Am I driven by these vestigial memories, this junk DNA that hangs on and makes me who I am?

He was in some form of ministry with people all his life, and now I am too. In Alabama, he and Mom ran a home for juvenile delinquent girls. He also worked as a prison chaplain and traveling preacher while he did construction work on the side. In Oregon, he was principal of a Christian school for two years. In Ohio, he taught at a Bible college for almost two decades. He and Mom always invited people into our home. A survivor of some serious abuse lived with us for thirteen years. It was all so normal. Now his normal is becoming my normal, and to draw from the wisdom of the *Princess Bride,* "I do not think that word means what you think it means."

I crashed in late January. By constantly overworking and studiously ignoring good advice, I managed to catch what I thought was the flu, but I couldn't shake it. Several days in bed turned into a week, and the following couple of weeks were characterized by a near inability to function. I dragged myself off to my part-time gig at school for two hours, then home and into bed for as much of the rest of the day as I could. I couldn't walk up the stairs without my legs shaking. I slept and slept and generally felt like crap.

Multiple doctors' visits, including several fun visits with needles and other unmentionable probes, managed to find nothing, but these visits did enable my doctor to get to know me better than I had originally planned. Medically, I was fine. I just couldn't function anymore.

A month stretched endlessly, six weeks. One day my better half pointed out the exhausted elephant in the room: "You're burned out."

I think I had this coming for six years. One way to keep death and failure and irrelevance seemingly at bay is through busyness.

Genesis tells me that the sin crouching at my door desires to master me. That's bad enough. I'm supposed to take comfort in God's presence: "Satan desires to sift you like wheat," said Jesus to Peter, "but I have prayed that your faith may not fail." But in life's dark valleys, where God becomes murky in the shadows, sometimes I get confused and wonder why it's God who is crouching at my door, and I think that the sifting has left more chaff in me than wheat.

I have a solution of sorts. If I can just be indispensable; if I can just be relevant all the time everywhere; if I can just maximize every waking moment; if I can Just. Keep. Going. Then not only will people need me, but maybe God will need me, too.

Then maybe He will let me stick around longer than He did my father, who was apparently not important enough to make it out of his fifties.

Then maybe my boys will not have to see their father shrivel into irrelevance.

Maybe Def Leppard was right (I, child of the 80s, told myself): it really is better to burn out than fade away. Turn it up; go for broke; watch my life go up in smoke.

> "COME TO ME, ALL YOU WHO ARE WEARY AND HEAVY LADEN AND I WILL GIVE YOU REST. TAKE MY YOKE UPON YOU FOR MY YOKE IS EASY AND MY BURDEN IS LIGHT.." DON'T WORRY—I AM NOT PREACHING AT YOU, I CERTAINLY HAVE HAD MY SHARE OF SIGNIFICANT DISILLUSIONMENT WITH GOD. FUNNY THOUGH, HE NEVER ACTUALLY TURNS OUT TO BE WHO I THOUGHT HE WAS. THANKS FOR SHARING, I'M GLAD WE'RE IN IT TOGETHER.
> —JAK

November 25, 2008

We drove to Uncle Bob and Aunt Joyce's for Thanksgiving. They had graciously allowed us to meet Chad (my cousin) and his wife Rachel (my wife's sister) at their home. I was glad to be there: I had been looking to connect more closely with Dad's family in the past couple of years, either as a substitute for his absence or as a long overdue recognition of the great legacy I have. Aunt Joyce is one degree of separation from Dad, which is pretty close. Plus, their whole family makes me laugh.

Thanksgiving was a good day but a hard day. Holidays are always hard now. They are better if they include long walks alone, a couple beers with friends, and a football game that does not include the Lions.

I wrote a poem that night, but I don't remember doing it. It is dated Thanksgiving Day, so I assume that date is true. I didn't have access to wireless that day, so I don't think I could have ripped it off from somewhere else; I don't know why I would have anyway. My best guess is that I had gone to bed and taken 10 milligrams of Ambien, a sleep aid I had been using so that I could stop dreading the ongoing specter of sleepless nights.

Trouble is, Ambien is a memory thief. The post-Ambien experience is simultaneously soothing ("Yay! I will actually sleep tonight!") and deceptive ("Of course you are lucid!"). This poem apparently rose from somewhere deep inside, unbidden, freed by a drug that protects sleep but destroys inhibitions. It captures what I had been feeling on and off for years since Dad's death, but never really had the guts to say.

So take it for what it was: the raw, unfiltered thoughts of a lonely son who—on Thanksgiving Day, late at night, staying up alone in a quiet farmhouse, sitting next to a sleeping wife who tried to empathize but could not fully do so no matter how hard she tried—really missed his dad. Missed him so much that death momentarily did not lurk threateningly in the shadows, as an enemy and thief who comes to steal this precious gift of life. "To die is gain," says the Good Book, and this was one of many times I have understood that verse as only those who have lost a loved one can.

LONELY
(Thanksgiving 2008)

My fountainhead shriveled, dried up in his bed.
With my tears I watered the grave of the dead
then staggered back home,
a few miles too far from a father who loved me,
and who is not anymore.

Now my life's stream is shrinking, losing its flow.
My source has dried up; where now do I go?
A wraith with a sickle stole peace, joy, and love
And no hope replenishes me from above.

If death were not sneaky, we would meet, He and I;
If death were not cold I would greet him.
If death were not always in hymnals and songs, we
would not need to honor him quite so damn long.

But death is a bastard who aims for our souls;
Our lives he despises while deep rivers roll.
And he's cold in his heart
and as fierce as a fire,
And yet I,
on this day,
give him all my desire.

"Webers, Thanksgiving, 2008"

*For more on <u>Pain and Hardship</u>, see page 105.

THE AFTERMATH: YEAR SEVEN

Faith is a gift; clarity is terrifying.
—John Rueben

April 2009

With Dad already gone, I experienced the end of Grandpa's life journey differently than I expected.

A couple of months before Grandpa died, my wife, my kids, and I met him and Grandma and some uncles and aunts in Midland, Michigan, for supper at Big Boy. After supper, Grandpa pulled me aside and very matter-of-factly said something along the lines of, "I wanted to meet you for supper because I don't have much more time." I think he was ready to go home. I know he was ready by the end.

I cried as I talked with Sheila on the drive home from Midland, but I was glad for Grandpa. After a lifetime, "Well done,

> I OFTEN THINK OF THE REUNION OF MY DAD AND HIS FIRST-BORN SON AND WONDER WHAT THEY WOULD TELL US NOW. I THINK IT MAY BE AS YOU HAVE FOUND OUT TO TRUST THE SOVEREIGN GOD.
> —MY DAD'S SISTER, MARY JANE

good and faithful servant, enter into the joy of the Lord" was not that far away. Good for you, Grandpa. May my life be one of your eulogies too.

Grandpa moved from Lancaster, Pennsylvania, to Atmore, Alabama, after he received a clear vision from God one day while he was driving a tractor. He stopped, put his head on the steering wheel, and heard God say, "Move to Alabama and be a preacher." So off he went with his wife and seven kids.

They started in Alabama with thirty acres. He farmed while working with the local Native American tribes. Soon, he bought another 400 wooded acres, which took him two years to clear. Once the land was cleared, he tested the soil, added the right fertilizer, and farmed.

He grew tired of ordering inferior seed from other states, so he started his own seed business. He became a chaplain at a local prison. He started a ministry to ex-prisoners called New Life Foundation, which eventually became We Care. In the 1960s and 1970s, in the midst of a racially charged southern climate, he was the first white man to preach in an all-black church in Mobile, Alabama; one of the ex-prisoners who benefited

> *from his ministry was the first black man to set foot in an all-white church in Mobile.*
>
> *Grandpa was never one to shy away from a challenge.*

It's funny how history lurks behind us. When Dad died, Grandpa still stood between me and the eternal past. I had to step up and be the "man of the family," but at least one of the giants on whose shoulders I stood still supported me. When I got news that Grandpa had died, I realized I was down to ground level now, and history began breathing down my neck. The giants were all gone. Was I really qualified to stand alone? Who knew that a father and grandfather could stand so strongly between the void of eternity past and the great weight of the present?

I have learned that death simultaneously destroys and creates empathy. When my dad died, I primarily thought of myself. I thought of my mom and sister a little—after I finished pining for me—but in general, I stayed lost in my own newfound sense of loss. Grief was so overwhelming and new that I didn't know what to do.

But at Grandpa's funeral, I thought more about what my uncles and aunts were feeling now that they, too, had lost their father. Now my cousins and I had something in common: we had all lost a grandfather, just like my children had lost theirs. I knew the emotional storm that was coming—I knew how the abyss gapes hungrily at a funeral; how the viewing drains a month's worth of life; how the burial doesn't seem real but at the same time smites your soul like a hammer. I knew the range of emotions that were coming.

I would not have thought about all those things before my father died. If grief is a dark cloud, empathy is the silver lining.

When we buried Grandpa, we lowered a good man down into the rich, red, Alabama clay only a few plots away from my dad's grave. Afterwards, I borrowed an umbrella from my cousin Conrad and joined a wet, southern rainstorm as I sobbed uncontrollably by the grave of my father.

> *Before my senior season in basketball, my dad sat me down and gave me the following speech (I paraphrase): "Son, I think you put too much into basketball. Your identity is wrapped up in it. Since I want you to know*

that my love for you does not depend on how you do in basketball, I will not be attending most of your basketball games." Every Saturday he would ask me how I did, and he attended a couple of big games, but he usually stayed home.

People ask if I resented his decision. No, I don't. I didn't then (because I was too self-absorbed) and I don't now (because I get it).

A light bulb went on for me while on a mission trip at Pura Vida Missions in Costa Rica, and I didn't even need the back-up generator.

I am a person consumed by fear. I have become a "catastrophe thinker": whenever something goes wrong, I assume my whole life will implode, and I will lose everything.

I am constantly tense about the next thing that could go wrong, no matter how trivial. I am always thinking ahead: What could I screw up next? What will go wrong in this particular area of my life? I realized two things tonight: I had downplayed how fearful I really am, and I wasn't always this way.

I wasn't like this before Dad died.

He desperately tried to do the right thing; I suspect he was as God-haunted as I am. A couple of missteps overshadowed a lifetime of good decisions and sacrifice, and everything he built up came crashing down. In his last years, he was close to earning his doctorate in counseling, and he had seen some positive steps in a second career.

However, he never recovered from going from a perennially popular Bible college teacher and student counselor to being a bellhop at night and cutlery salesman during the day. It was a rough way to end a good life.

Is it any surprise I think of catastrophes?

I am afraid to go to bed, because I will have a terrible time sleeping.

I am afraid of this next week here, because the staff has planned a lot of unexpected things.

I am afraid that this trip will not be successful.

I am afraid I will gain weight this week.

I am afraid that something will happen to Sheila and me, or to the boys.

I am afraid I won't be able to prepare my sermon in time for the first week that we are back.

I am afraid I am a screw-up as a youth pastor.

> I AM AFRAID THAT AT SOME POINT I WILL BE BOLD ENOUGH TO BE JUST AS OPEN AND HONEST ABOUT MY PAIN AND FEARS AS YOU HAVE BEEN, AND THE RESPONSE WILL BE ... <CRICKETS>.
> —BG

I am afraid our stupid dog Trixie will escape
from our backyard while we are gone.
I am afraid my next sermon will bomb.
I am afraid our schools will close.
I am afraid I completely misunderstand heaven and hell.
I am afraid I have gotten two degrees that will utterly fail me.
I am afraid I am stupid, and I only think I am smart.
I am afraid I am creepy.
I am afraid I will screw up our marriage,
which would also mean I screw up
my family and my current career.
I am afraid Sheila will stop loving me.
I am afraid I am a bad parent, and I
am loading my boys with baggage.
I am afraid my new
brown shoes are too loud
for every outfit I brought to Costa Rica.
I am afraid someday I will find out Christianity is not what I think it is.
I am afraid I have offended people who aren't telling
me, and they are slowly building resentment.
I am afraid all kinds of other people are disappointed with me.

> DOES EVERYONE FEEL LIKE THAT WHEN THEY LOSE SOMEONE THEY LOVE, OR JUST SOME PEOPLE? JUST WONDERIN'.
> —DM

When my kids were young, they jumped off things—couches, beds, tree limbs, deck railings, bunk beds—and just expected me to catch them, even if it meant throwing my forty-year-old back into next week. They couldn't even conceive that I wouldn't be there. Their eyes glowed with happiness, because Daddy was catching them. Their jumps embodied the trust in their heart, because I. Would. Be. Ready. They trusted me completely. They jumped again … and again … and again … and again … In the end, all was well (except for my aching shoulders), and they slept soundly that night, because Daddy caught them until they were done jumping.

> THIS ONE GOT ME …. I TOO HAVE OFTEN HAD A LOT OF THOSE SAME FEELINGS OVER THE LAST SEVEN YEARS.
> —AKA

I don't think I trust anyone, because the one I am supposed to trust the most—

the one who is supposed to catch me when I jump—allowed death to take my father on a Tuesday night in January. The light bulb in Costa Rica on this windy mountain evening shines off of eyes that do not return the glow; the wavering shadows around me betray my faltering heart.

One time, at a hotel pool, Vincent jumped into the deep end over and over, because I was there to catch him before he went under. He was kind of scared, but because I was there, he got over his fear. He even tried to run away from me and jump, thinking it was clever, but he scared me. One day he will jump when I am not there, not realizing that the water has the power to rob him of at least his trust, and perhaps his life.

Vincent and I.

Six years ago, I jumped—no, even worse, I was pushed—into the deep end of life. And while I know that God was there—I know this, in my head—I did not feel his arms catch me. And the deep end was much deeper than I anticipated.

God, you know all things, so you know this already.

I am not sure when I will jump again.

* **For more thoughts on <u>God</u>, go to page 109.**

Sooner or later He withdraws ... all those supports and incentives. He leaves the creature to stand up on its own legs—to carry out from the will alone duties which have lost all relish. It is during such trough periods, much more than during the peak periods, that it is growing into the sort of creature He wants it to be. Hence the prayers offered in the state of dryness are those which please Him best.

We can drag our patients along by continual tempting, because we design them only for the table, and the more their will is interfered with the better. He cannot "tempt" to virtue as we do to vice. He wants them to learn to walk and must therefore take away His hand; and if only the will to walk is really there He is pleased even with their stumbles. Do not be deceived, Wormwood. Our cause is never more in danger than when a human, no longer desiring, but still intending, to do our Enemy's will, looks round upon a universe from which every trace of Him seems to have vanished, and asks why he has been forsaken, and still obeys.

—C. S. Lewis, *The Screwtape Letters*

October 2009

I know people mean well. They try to be optimistic and never speak negatively about anything; they always speak as if everything will be all right. That's great, but—sorry, this has be said—that's a stupid way to view the world. It's a bad reading of Scripture, and it's a bad analysis of life. Ask the disciples. Ask Job. Ask Jesus. *(Jesus: "Let this cup pass from me!" God, in a thundering voice: "How dare you speak about this negative cup! What is wrong with you? Now you have to die!")*

Half of my baggage was piled on by well-meaning but ignorant people. Can you imagine Peter telling Jesus, "Don't forget what God said: I know the plans I have for you, plans to prosper you and not to harm you"? I'm pretty sure—stop me if I'm wrong here—that Jesus was under so much duress he sweated blood and begged God for an alternative plan, and God said no.

That was why I prayed for my dad, but always finished with, "Not my will, but yours be done."

The world is probably better if God's will trumps mine.

How does prayer work again? Tons of people prayed for my dad, and he *died*. I understand the principle behind both sovereignty and free will, but I am less certain than ever that I understand how they exist in tension. Does it make sense that I don't even want to pray? Is God okay with me getting ready to pray and then thinking, "What's the point?" We live and die, we laugh and cry; that much I know with certainty, but after that, it gets murky. Everything else seems like a matter of guesswork. "Hope" is the good Christian word I should use instead, I suppose, but "guesswork" captures how I feel at this moment with much greater clarity.

I know God wants us to pray; I know prayer matters. It's just that after so many prayers from so many godly people did not bring what seemed like such an obvious solution for my dad, I don't know why I should pray. Clearly a sovereign God overrode us. That's cool; that's His prerogative. I'm not angry anymore. It just makes the relationship feel one-sided.

I don't have to get it on this side of heaven, but I sure wish I could. I am still running the race, and this prayer hurdle still trips me up a lot. I pray the Lord's Prayer almost all the time now, or at least variations of it.

Jesus himself said, "Pray like this," so at least I know we're on the same side on this prayer.

Is God honored that I pray because I know I should, not because I want to? Is that a prayer of faith? Is it a sign of faith that I plug away because I believe in and trust Him above all others, even if I don't understand Him?

ONE TIME I HAD A CONVERSATION WITH GOD. I WAS SAYING, "YA KNOW, GOD, I THOUGHT HE WAS GONNA BE HEALED. I THOUGHT WE WERE GONNA GET TO GROW OLD TOGETHER...TO TRAVEL AND ENJOY EACH OTHER AND WORK TOGETHER TO BRING YOUR KINGDOM TO EARTH." HE ANSWERED ME, "I KNOW ... THAT IS WHAT I WANTED TOO." I NEVER HAD THAT CONVERSATION WITH HIM AGAIN, BUT I LOVED HIM ALL THE MORE.
—MB

YOU ARE TAKING ME BACK TO MEMORIES I WOULD PREFER SCARRED OVER AND LEFT THAT WAY.... I LIVE THERE MORE THAN I CARE TO ADMIT. DOES EVERYONE FEEL LIKE THAT WHEN THEY LOSE SOMEONE THEY LOVE, OR JUST SOME PEOPLE? JUST WONDERIN'.
—DSM

I HAVE ASKED GOD MANY TIMES, OVER THE SIXTEEN YEARS SINCE DAD SUFFERED THE STROKE, WHEN HE WAS GOING TO HEAL MY DAD AND HE ALWAYS SAYS, "TRUST ME." I GUESS IF NOT IN THIS LIFE, FOR SURE IN THE NEXT WE WILL KNOW. BUT THEN, I GUESS IT REALLY WON'T MATTER, WILL IT?
—CJ

*For more on <u>Prayer,</u> see page 112.

THE AFTERMATH: YEAR EIGHT

O, Lord, do not rebuke me in your anger, nor chasten me in
your hot displeasure. Have mercy on me, O Lord, for I am
weak; O Lord, heal me, for my bones are troubled. My soul
is greatly troubled; But you, O Lord—how long? Return, O
Lord, deliver me! Oh, save me for your mercies' sake!

Psalm 38:1–4, NKJV

July 2010. Costa Rica. Again.

There is a difference between knowing God and knowing about God.

I know basketball; I know *about* MMA.

I know my friends Karl and Scott; I know *about* President Obama.

I know nachos; I know *about* caviar.

> **Welcome to the fallout ... the tension is here, between who you are and who you could be.**
> **—Switchfoot**

To know about something, I just have to be aware of its existence. Maybe I even appreciate it (caviar), or enjoy and cheer it (MMA), or recognize its impact on the world (President Obama). But to really know something, I have to experience it; I have to invest emotional, spiritual, mental, and maybe even physical stock. I had to have taken a chance on the market and decided the risk was worth the investment, and then buckled up and gone along for the ride.

It is a life in which much can be gained and much can be lost. I can become wealthy or impoverished depending on the wisdom of my investment, and it can happen in a day or a lifetime.

After thirty-five years of believing and following and seeking to be like Him, I think today I know a lot about God, more than I actually know Him.

I think about God, but I don't often feel Him. I try to follow His paths, but I often don't see His heart. I try to live by His priorities, but only because I believe they are true and good, not because I am always excited about living that way.

Believing in God intellectually? That I can do. I appreciate, enjoy, and cheer His existence; I see and like His impact on the world. But embracing Him and experiencing Him? That's a different game for me altogether.

I have invested in Him. I have put my stock in Him for about thirty-five years. Granted, some years I invested lightly, but other years I mortgaged the farm. I put heart, soul, mind, and strength into GodStock.

Intellectually, stock is up! Perhaps more than ever, the claim that God exists and has revealed Himself through Jesus and in the Bible is more supportable than ever.

Emotionally, I have been devastated at times. There was the death of my father, dead of pancreatic cancer at fifty-seven, whose ghost still lingers.

Physically, I've been often ill from mysterious maladies. I apparently have not been given the physical fortitude to support my ministry.

Spiritually, I've been dry. God feels as distant from me as the Lions are from playing in the Super Bowl.

Mentally, I have been tormented by the scars of past sins and overwhelmed by the songs of the American Sirens beckoning me to taste and see that the world is good.

> **Faithless is he that says farewell when the road darkens.**
> **J. R. R. Tolkien, *The Fellowship of the Ring***

I have made my peace in the willful, volitional part of my nature. I can still do the right things. But the rest of me has taken a beating. Ironically, God's presence was more real than ever at times in the midst of my mourning, but my experience of that presence has not lasted. I'm at the point that I almost wish for another death to bring His reality closer to me again.

But why must that connection with God be forged in the furnace of pain? "All creation groans in agony"; why must that be the price? Why? I don't really want someone to die so that in the midst of the crushing grief God and I can be tight again. That can't be the formula, right? Right?

My own words condemn me. I preached the following in a sermon not long after Dad's death:

> *"I have often heard comments along the line of, 'I wish God would reveal Himself to me. I wish I could hear from God.' I know what people mean. There have been times in my life when God felt very real and close—oddly enough in the immediacy of my father's death, God felt very close. His peace was at times almost tangible, and I experienced dreams that were unlike any other in my life, during which I received some closure with my dad. But it wasn't too long before He did not feel that way at all. In fact, He seemed very absent and stubbornly quiet when I prayed and read Scripture.*

> *"But He wasn't, actually. God's silence was more a reflection of how I felt. He spoke to me through my wife, and my mentors, and books, and music. I wanted more dreams, and I wanted an encounter or an experience that felt supernatural, but God very stubbornly and persistently spoke to me in less obvious ways. God speaks ... it's just that often the message isn't sent the way I want it to be or expect it to be."*

Am I the problem? I have tried so hard to turn my back on my past sins; I have committed myself to "forgetting what lies behind and pressing on." So why does the past still press so closely behind me? The Son shines on me, but I still hear the footsteps of temptation in my shadow, and the harder I run, the louder the footsteps ring. I would turn to rebuke my pursuer, but I'm afraid I might not look away.

Part of the frustration is that I'm really, really trying to follow God's path for life because I believe it is the only way to go, but I still live in turmoil. My health constantly suffers; I am driven 24/7 by the need to maximize my life, with the result that I have apparently no ability to relax; I am judgmental in spite of all the things for which I have been forgiven; I struggle with a sense of entitlement, with pride, with discontent.

Is this life more abundant? Is this the promise? What am I missing?

Most importantly, is God okay with a man who believes in Him because of who He is; who outwardly lives for Him because that is the right thing to do; but who has a hellish time making his heart join in with his head and his hands?

I wonder if this affects my marriage more than I realize. If my relationship with God is connected to my relationship with my wife—Paul talks about the "mystery" of marriage being like Christ and the church—should it surprise me if I feel the same dynamic in my marriage?

I feel like I have withdrawn from my wife. Is it because my skin and soul are connected? Has my discontentment with my relational investment with God spilled over into other areas of my life?

The list goes on, of course. I withhold from everyone and everything. Investment is hard. The greater the risk, the greater the potential reward, beauty and life. But the greater the risk, the greater the potential for hurt, for disillusionment, for pain.

I guess that, as with God, I expect them to disappoint me. What has happened before may happen again, with all of them. History feels, some days, like destiny. There have been so many good, meaningful times, but there have been bad times as well. I am supposed to let the good times build momentum to crash through the bad, but sometimes speed makes the crash hurt worse. Maybe, if I were going more slowly, the inevitable would feel more manageable.

My wife, my friends, people around me ... do they deserve my disappointment and withdrawal? Even if they do, am I somehow justified? It's not as if I haven't disappointed them. And even if I have been genuinely disappointed, and my feelings are justified, is the answer really to pull back? To become clinical and detached? To pull out of friendships in case a pleasant dip in the cool water of connection threatens to drown me?

I know the answer: "Withdrawal is a way of escaping the hard, beautiful, costly, rewarding, gritty, and wonderful reality of a life lived in community and relationship. When you withhold yourself, you deny your humanity and diminish the image of God in yourself and in others." I know about that answer, and I fully agree with it. I just want to experience it; feel it; embrace it in the core of my being.

W. H. Auden said it well: "We who must die demand a miracle."

THOSE WHO KNOW YOUR NAME ("THE TOTAL PERSON, PERSONALITY, AND RELIABLE CHARACTER OF GOD") WILL PUT THEIR TRUST IN YOU.

—PSALM 9:9–10

OH, TASTE ("CHOOSE AND DELIGHT") AND SEE THAT THE LORD IS GOOD. BLESSED IS THE MAN WHO TRUSTS IN HIM.

—PSALM 34:8

*For more on Embracing Life, see page 115.

THE AFTERMATH: TODAY

I have been authentic before God, exposing maybe the worst part of myself. And somehow, God was accepting me with all of that. I think I "made space" for God to pour grace into me. And God will come if there is space.
—Phillip Yancey

Though I am lowly, I do not forget your words.
—Psalm 119:141

March 2010

Today, I am more comforted by my faith than ever before. Here is the odd part: I am comforted intellectually. My feelings took a beating, so I'm giving them some time off, but I am more confident than ever that my faith is grounded in reality and truth. Even when God has felt distant, I have seen his wisdom in his guidance for life. My job allows me to hear the stories of many people, and if there is one thing that is becoming increasingly clear, it is that the path of God is the only path that offers a correct diagnosis and a cure for the world. I have noticed a distinct trend: when people live in a way God said not to live, their lives spiral downward relentlessly. When people follow God's advice, they avoid a ton of physical, emotional, and intellectual hardship. It doesn't mean "Make God your choice and you get a Rolls Royce." It just means that, practically speaking, God knows best. I am glad I can see the truth of His ways, even if I don't always understand Him.

> Not all who wander are lost.
> — Tolkien

May I always remember:

That God is good, even when life is not.
That He is near, even when
I don't feel Him.
That He is watching, even
when my eyes are closed.
That He is not silent, even when I
silence him with distractions.
That He is not hidden, even
when I cannot see Him.
That death wins one battle with
everyone, but not the war.
That my father did not stop living;
he just stopped living here.

> "HE JUST STOPPED LIVING HERE." THIS IS THE PROMISE/HOPE MY HEART CLINGS TO. THAT MY MOTHER'S NEW HEART BEATS STRONG AND HER LAUGHTER RINGS OUT LOUD AND CLEAR.... THIS HOPE/VISION DRIES MY TEARS MOST DAYS.
> —GOB

Today, I am praying again. Not because I have it all figured out, but in spite of that fact. Slowly, something is rebuilding with me, and it whispers ever so quietly that God is near, and He wishes for me to speak to Him. I am back to the basics: The Lord's Prayer. I am plumbing the depths of that one as I get my prayer legs back under me. I recently read a book about how prayer humbles us, as it reminds us every time that life is out of our control. I need to pray if for no other reason than to remind myself that I. Need. God.

August 2010

While sitting on my back deck with me this morning, my five-year-old, Vincent, said, out of the blue, "Why can't I see Grandpa?"

"Because Grandpa isn't here."

"But when can we go see him? We can drive."

"Because Grandpa is in heaven. He is not anywhere we can go visit him right now."

A little contemplation, then, "But when can we go visit him?"

"When we get to heaven, then we can visit him again. We will get to see him there."

"Okay," he said very matter-of-factly, and off he ran to pet the goldfish in our outdoor pond.

It is easy to forget the comfort of heaven, and the hope that comes with it. Is it really as simple as my five-year-old makes it? "I can't see him now. Oh, that's right. Heaven. Got it." Off he runs to embrace the beautiful, broken world that is still around him. Grandpa is okay; one day Vincent will join him. For now, the goldfish need visiting. Life is good. All will be well.

When AJ and I had the same discussion about a year after Dad's death, we were standing in the front yard. The topic came up out of the blue then too, and the conversation was almost identical, except AJ finished with, "Then I want to go to heaven now."

I gently tried to explain that he would have to die first, a connection he had not made before. But even then I could see the conflict on his face: life is good, but heaven looks really good too. That's a lot for an eight-year-old to process.

And now, today, I am lying in bed as I write this, blood thinners coursing through my veins, trying to take it easy so I don't dislodge a blood clot in my lower right leg. A diagnosis of a torn calf muscle turned out to be a mistake, and off I went to the ER Monday night to keep my lungs, heart, and brain safe. I am taking drugs and lying in bed to make sure I don't get a pulmonary embolism and, well, die.

It's funny how suddenly mortality looms. What is simply a sad part of life when it happens to others becomes personal quickly.

But I have discovered that something I believed in theory has been challenged by reality, and the theory holds up: I am not afraid to die. When I think of my own mortality, I think of the impact on my wife, my kids, the youth kids that I coach, and teach, and hang out with, and love. I get emotional over them, but not over me.

It's not because I'm spiritually awesome. I think it's because as I worked through my dad's demise, something settled within me. Heaven is his home; it's mine too. To die really is to gain. It took Christ's crucifixion to show the world that death has been swallowed up in victory; it took my dad's death to bring it home to me.

The following phrase may never appear in print again: *I am going to think like Vincent.* Dad is okay; one day I will join him. For now, the world needs visiting. Life is good. All will be well.

Dad, I will see you again, but not yet.

Not yet.

Weber Family, 2010

"You do not yet look as happy as I mean you to be."

Lucy said, "We're so afraid of being sent away, Aslan. And you have sent us back into our own world so often."

"No fear of that," said Aslan. "Have you not guessed?" Their hearts leaped and a wild hope rose within them.

"There was a real railway accident," said Aslan softly. "Your father and mother and all of you are—as you used to call it in the Shadowlands—dead. The term is over: the holidays have begun. The dream is over: this is the morning."

And as He spoke He no longer looked to them like a lion; but the things that began to happen after that were so great and beautiful that I cannot write them. And for us this is the end of all the stories, and we can most truly say that they all lived happily ever after.

But for them it was only the beginning of the real story. All their life in this world and all their adventures in Narnia had only been the cover and the title page: now at last they were beginning Chapter One of the Great Story, which no one on earth has ever read: which goes on for ever: in which every chapter is better than the one before.

—C. S. Lewis, *The Last Battle*

MOVING BEYOND THE MEMORIES

CONFRONTING LIFE

In my experience, the Western Christian church has trouble facing life honestly. Life is clearly full of valleys and shadows, but I hear so many conversations and read so many books in which attempts are made to pretend that valleys are actually plains, and shadows are illusions.

This denial manifests in "name it and claim it" silliness; "God wants me to be happy" shallowness; and "if I have enough faith, nothing can harm me" wistfulness. These distortions deny the absolutely clear realities about life we know from Scripture:

> *We will have trouble (John 16:33)*
> *The Lord gives and takes away (Job 1:21)*
> *God does not always relieve us of our struggle (2 Corinthians 12:7–10)*
> *The world is more like Gethsemane than Eden*
> *right now (Genesis 2; Matthew 26)*
> *Even Jesus felt deserted by God (Mark 15:34)*
> *Everybody dies (Hebrews 9:27)*
> *Everybody ought to mourn (Ecclesiastes 3)*
> *Sometimes bad things happen (Luke 13:4)*
> *Even godly people can be poor and sickly (Book of Job)*

We civilized Western Christians are desperate to make our lives safe and easy and comfortable, so we convince ourselves that God, too, wants our lives to be a walk and whistle through the park.

Why do we have such trouble facing reality head on? Do we think God isn't big enough to sustain us? Do we think we are too weak for the task? Do we think that struggle equates to failure? Whatever the reason, a lot of us "duck and cover" our way through life. If it is true that ideas have consequences, then it follows that this denial of reality cannot be believed without consequences.

In our attempts to sidestep the real world, we lay claim to an imaginary world, and we convince ourselves to believe things that we shouldn't. Since, as Christians, our foundation is the Bible, it makes sense that our imaginary world finds its foundation in imaginary messages and ideas we get by misreading and misapplying biblical verses like the following:

You will have none of these diseases (Exodus 15:26)
By His stripes you are healed (Isaiah 53:5)
I know the plans I have for you, plans to prosper you
and not to harm you… (Jeremiah 29:11)
All things work together for good to those who love God (Romans 8:28)

Never mind that the first has to do with the dietary and hygienic changes the Israelites were going to implement after leaving Egypt, or that the second has to do with the healing of sin, or that the "plan" in Jeremiah was for the Israelites in captivity in Babylon, or that "all things working out" refers to our spiritual redemption. An imaginary world where we will always be happy and disease-free requires an imaginative reading of the Bible.

One of the hardest things for me to do after Dad's death was to process all the uber-positive messages I kept hearing from the imaginary world. People sent us notes or read one of the above verses to us over the phone. They exhibited a remarkable ability to rip the Bible out of context—and out of reality as well. Even though everyone had good intentions, good intentions have paved some pretty depressing roads.

When someone says, "God gave me this verse for you," and the message of that verse does not happen, there are three main options:

1. Your friends think they are hearing from God when they are not (which is a problem).
2. The Bible is written so obscurely as to be almost incomprehensible (bigger problem).
3. God lied.

We are immediately left with the first two options, at least if we want to keep our faith intact.

But if the transmitters of God's will are that faulty, what hope do we have that

> THIS IS A GOOD REMINDER THAT I NEED TO BE ANCHORED AND WALKING IN THE TRUTH, PERSONALLY, AND READING THE WORD THROUGH GOD'S EYES, NOT THE COLORED LENSES I MAY WANT TO WEAR ON ANY GIVEN DAY.
> —MS

we can hear from Him correctly? If the Bible is that murky, and all God's people are that deluded, is it any wonder that Christians often struggle with their faith after times of calamity?

The dilemma in trying to balance our faith with these options is that the list of options is not complete. Even though they feel like the only choices we have, I believe there are more.

I don't believe God lies; I don't believe His Word is so obscure as to be incomprehensible; I don't believe His people are so fallen as to never hear His voice. I do believe, however, that in an attempt to make the world like we desperately want it to be, we read parts of the Bible from a perspective that is tainted by our fallen, selfish nature.

The Bible has not failed us; we have failed it. We treat it like a magic lamp: if we can rub it just right, God will pop out and grant us wishes. We spend a lot of time and energy reading books and going to seminars on Genie Control; we hear Christina Aguilera sing "Genie in a Bottle" and mistake if for a praise song. We criticize Harry Potter for wanting to use magic to fix his problems, then we go to Christian Hogwarts to find a magic wand that will put the perfect life just one good spell—sorry, prayer—away.

The unfortunate result is that when God fails to respond to our frantic efforts, we blame Him … or, if that is too brazen, we blame others. Even worse, we can become like the prophets of Baal and perform increasingly demanding and self-damaging acts of piety in a desperate attempt to get God's attention.

Why do we think God must give liberty to our passions? Why does it follow that if we hurt, or we endure hardship, that God automatically must be mean?

The Apostle Paul said that when we become adults, we have to stop being like children, and that includes our thinking about the hard roads in life. Here's the bottom line:

> WHAT A REFRESHING … AND WONDERFUL REMINDER THAT WE LIVE IN A FALLEN WORLD WITH REAL HURTS, REAL TRIALS, AND A REAL GOD THAT IS GOOD.
> —JTF

IF WE MISUNDERSTAND GOD'S WORDS, WE WILL MISUNDERSTAND
GOD'S WORLD; IF WE MISUNDERSTAND GOD'S WORLD, WE
WILL MISUNDERSTAND GOD; IF WE MISUNDERSTAND GOD, WE
MISUNDERSTAND THE SOURCE OF THE HOPE WITHIN US.

EMOTIONS

We live in a culture that is far more emotive than intellectual. Watch reality shows for a while, then listen to the top 100 songs on the radio, then ask yourself how much of the presentation appeals to the intellect and how much appeals to the emotions. Unfortunately, this same culture disconnects the proper emotional response from the facts of the event. We have a hard time feeling what we are supposed to feel.

This is not a new problem. When Jesus was trying to describe the generation of his time, He used this analogy: "We played a wedding song, and you did not dance; we played a funeral dirge, and you did not mourn" (Matthew 11:17). The people didn't rejoice when they should have been happy, and they didn't mourn when they should have grieved.

This was not Jesus lecturing pompously from some golden ethereal throne. He "was found in the fashion of a man"; he was an emotional person.

"Where have you put him?" he asked them. They told him, "Lord, come and see." And Jesus <u>wept</u>. The people standing nearby said, "See how much He <u>loved</u> him." (John 11:34–36, NLT)
"He was despised and rejected—a man of <u>sorrows</u>, acquainted with deepest <u>grief</u>." (Isaiah 53:3, NLT)
"As he approached Jerusalem and saw the city, He <u>wept</u> over it." (Luke 19:41, NIV).
<u>"Rejoice</u> with me, for I have found my sheep which was lost." (Luke 15:6, ESV)
Other passages refer to His <u>grief</u> (Ephesians 4:30), <u>anger</u> (John 2:15), <u>outrage</u> (Hebrews 10:29), and <u>love</u> (1 John 4:8).

As a culture, I don't think we are very good with death. We sing songs about being "forever young"; we suspend ourselves in adolescent behavior for as long as we can; we tolerate injections and pop pills; we exercise, cleanse, and endure diets to hold off the persistence of time. When people die, we grieve so briefly and so privately compared to many other cultures around the world.

Here's the reality: our minds were damaged by sin. We don't naturally think about the world the way God thinks about the world. In the same way, our emotions were damaged by sin, and we don't naturally feel about the world the way God feels about the world. Our head and our heart need to be transformed into the image of Christ.

This emotional transformation isn't often discussed. Growing up Mennonite, I don't remember hearing a lot about emotions. The children of Menno try really hard to live right and do right; what we feel about something doesn't make the radar screen from the pulpit or in the pew. WWJD was the perfect bracelet. Nobody would have worn WWJF. What Jesus felt seemed to matter far less than what Jesus did.

Now that I am in a nondenominational, more charismatic church, there is more of an openness to the interplay of emotion and faith. While this awareness is good, it is not without its downside: people can feel obligated to display emotions that don't mirror what they are really feeling inside.

The Western church is pretty good at rejoicing at the right time. Everybody loves a party. We celebrate weddings, babies, sobriety, potlucks, Thomas Kinkaid, salvation, and movies with Kirk Cameron. But, unlike a lot of our fellow Christians who live in areas of the world that are far more brutal than ours, we haven't really embraced what it means to "weep with

> I WILL GO IN WITH YOU TO DESIGN THE WWJF BRACELET :) TOO MANY TIMES WHEN SOMEONE IS IN EMOTIONAL PAIN (WHETHER IT IS FROM THE SICKNESS OR DEATH OF A LOVED ONE, THE ABUSE OR NEGLECT OF A LOVED ONE, OR SOMETHING ELSE), THEY ARE ENCOURAGED ... TO PUT A GOOD FACE ON IT AND NOT THINK OR FEEL A CERTAIN WAY. BUT THE REALITY IS THAT WHAT JESUS DOES WHEN HIS PEOPLE ARE IN PAIN IS WEEP, AND WHEN THE PERSON IN PAIN IS ABLE TO SEE THAT, THERE IS MUCH HEALING.
> —TS

those who weep." We are back to that imaginary world. If we can just paste on smiles, and say only happy words, then all *must* be well. It *must.*

If you are a follower of Christ, there are several things you probably believe:

Life as we know it is going to end.
It will hurt at some point.
There is life on the other side, better and different than this one.

We know these things to be true, but in spite of all the times we say that the grave has no sting and death has no victory, we don't live and feel like we really believe that. People close to us have died and it stung, and it sure seemed like death won the day. What do we do about this disconnect?

I don't think the verse is wrong. I think we misunderstand the point. The "sting and victory of death" in the Bible does not refer to the event or the emotions associated with it as much as it refers to the outcome. Does death have the final word? No. Jesus does. "It is finished" when He says it is finished. The hope of eternity offsets the momentary sting of loss, and the victory of Christ's resurrection overrides the "victory" of death.

> It is of the very essence of Christianity to face suffering and death not because they are good, not because they have meaning, but because the resurrection of Jesus has robbed them of their meaning.
> —Thomas Merton

The biggest hurdle isn't knowing this in our head or believing it in our hearts; the biggest hurdle is feeling it in our soul.

When the flood of emotions hit during Dad's decline and after his death, I didn't know what to do. I knew what to think, but I wasn't sure what my heart was supposed to feel. Looking back, I don't think there was a right or wrong to how I felt. How I responded to those feelings mattered more.

Earning my degree in theology before Dad died gave me plenty of time to intellectually accept that grief/pain and God are compatible. The philosophical problem of evil is not as problematic as it once was, not just in the ivory castles of philosophers but also in the recesses of my own mind. But until Dad died, I never wanted to look death in the face and pull it in close to my heart; it was just too final, too hard, too life-altering.

But now, now that I have seen my root cut out, and I realize there are still green shoots, I know I can survive.

That's actually a relief. When I die, people will grieve—my sons will have to chart their own path through the valley I have walked through, but they, too, by the grace of God, will survive. Lately, while praying for the healing of a very elderly and very sick acquaintance, I thought clearly, for maybe the first time ever, "Let him go. He needs to go home."

We fear death because we believe that life is over. It certainly appears that way. But in those months and years following Dad's death, at the times when death itself seemed to be the most daunting, I was always reminded that death is not the end. If I could just anticipate what kind of new life waited for me on the other side of the veil, I would be a different man.

By the grace of God, I have caught a glimpse already, and the transformation has begun.

DREAMS

Scripture and science agree yet again: Our dreams are not to be dismissed too quickly. There is something very real about them.

Scripture first:

> *I will bless the Lord who has counseled me; Indeed, <u>my mind (inner man) instructs me in the night.</u> (Psalm 16:7, NASB)*

> *"For God speaks once, twice, yet men do not perceive it. <u>In a dream, in a vision of the night,</u> when deep sleep falls upon men while sleeping upon the bed, <u>then God opens the ears of men.</u>" (Job Job 33: 14–15)*

Science second:

> *"We dismiss dreams because they end when we wake up. However, the duration of the experience doesn't mean it has any less basis in physical reality. Certainly we don't think day-to-day life is less real because we fall asleep or die. It's true we don't remember events in our dreams as well as in waking hours, but the fact that Alzheimer's patients may have little memory of events doesn't mean their life is any less real.*
> *"We also dismiss dreams as unreal because they're associated with brain activity during sleep. But are our waking hours unreal because they're associated with the neural activity in our brain? Certainly, the bio-physical logic of consciousness—whether during a dream or waking hours—can always be traced backwards, whether to neurons or the Big Bang. But according to biocentrism, reality is a process that involves our consciousness.*
> *"Whether awake or dreaming, you're experiencing the same bio-physical process. True, they're qualitatively different realities, but if you're thinking and feeling, it's real."*
> —*Robert Lanzq*, Are Dreams an Extension of Physical Reality?

The ancients believed that when they dreamed, they were accessing a parallel real world in their dreams. Socrates and Plato believed dreams held prophetic truth; St. Augustine believed images in our dreams were so real they carried moral weight; Thomas Aquinas believed God could communicate with us in dreams. Rene Descartes decided no one could empirically show the difference between dreams and reality.

The rise of modernism and the machines gave us not only *Terminator* sequels but also the decline of the mystical. Immanuel Kant (and much later philosophers like Norman Malcolm) dismissed the significance of dreams completely. Two Harvard scientists, Allan Hobson and Rober McCarley, recently described dreams as "meaningless biology" with a "preprogrammed, neurally determined genesis."

Freud, among others, believed dreams were only meaningful in that they opened a window into the unconscious mind, displaying vivid re-enactments of repressed wishes. Jung tried to connect some deeper, archetypal meaning to dreams, but even that explanation had a hint of the "ghost in the machine."

The bottom line of modernism? We are all machines now. Everything is mechanical and hardwired; people are all gears and levers, fully explicable in terms of atoms and chemicals in motion.

I have to disagree.

I understand that our brain uses our sleep cycle to unload, and that our dream life can merely reflect the experiences of our waking hours. I'm not ignorant about these things.

While that explanation may be a necessary part of understanding the brain, I don't believe it's sufficient to explain how the brain works in its entirety. In REM sleep, activity increases in the thalamocortical region of the brain, the same area that engages when we are awake. The machines used to measure brain activity cannot tell the difference between the awake brain and the dreaming brain. We think and feel and see, we just can't respond physically.

Now, scientists are also studying "lucid dreams," where people know they are dreaming; they make choices and carry out previously made plans. The dreamers are intentional, emotive, and intelligent in an inner world that is not chaotic and random, but very organized and purposeful. Stephen LaBerge, who has been researching lucid dreaming for years at Stanford, wrote, "People may be able to use lucid dreaming to shorten the time it takes them to recover from illnesses or operations, and to stimulate the redevelopment of physical skills following an injury." He went on to say they found that "the effects of dream events on the brain and body are much more like the effects of real events" *(Lucidity Research, Past and Future)*.

What best accounts for all that we know about dreams? Are dreams the output of the modernist machines? Are they Jung's ethereal archetypes? Or does a parallel real world have a way of crossing the divide?

We have pulled apart the atom and seen light-years into space; we have sequenced DNA and mapped the movement of chemicals in our brains; we have formulated string theory and peeked into quantum physics. We have learned a lot, but we have forgotten a lot too. We are now aware that we know less than ever before. We believe so strongly in the ability of science to reduce reality to bytes and memes that we have forgotten how deep the rabbit hole really goes.

True, science has unveiled mysteries in the heavens and the earth. It does not follow that there are no more mysteries or that every corner of reality will eventually succumb to microscope and telescope.

In *A Skeptic's Guide to Faith*, Philip Yancey notes:

Metaphysics deals with the unseen, that slippery world of first principles and invisible forces and regenerated souls. Yet the books [a physicist friend] gives me on modern physics seem to me more metaphysical than anything I read in William James. I learn that consciousness plays a key role in physical reality, that quantum events depend on an outside observer, that measuring the spin of one particle may affect the spin of another billions of miles away, that string theory proposes as many as ten dimensions (or eleven, or maybe twenty-six) to explain how the forces of the universe work together, that parallel universes may exist which influence us in ways we cannot detect. In psychology, theology, and physics, the line separating the two worlds, physical and spiritual, is uncertain at best.

The novelist Dean Koontz uses the phrase "out of the corner of his eye" to describe a tantalizing part of reality that is fleeting, tantalizing, and mysterious, but very real.

Koontz wrote an entire novel with that same title to capture the idea that we are surrounded by a reality that transcends the ordinary. We will sometimes see things out of the corners of our eyes. There will be things in heaven and earth, Horatio, of which we have not dreamed.

Or maybe we have, after all.

"GOD, THIS IS BRENDA. I DON'T WANT HIM BACK … WELL, I DO, BUT I KNOW YOU CAN'T DO THAT. ONLY GIVE ME THE STRENGTH TO BEAR THIS, OKAY? AND I WONDER IF MAYBE … YOU COULD LET HIM TALK TO ME ONE MORE TIME … I KNOW YOU DON'T DEAL IN GHOSTS—EXCEPT, OF COURSE, FOR THE HOLY ONE—BUT MAYBE IN A DREAM? I KNOW IT'S A LOT TO ASK, BUT … OH, GOD, THERE'S SUCH A HOLE IN ME TONIGHT. I DIDN'T KNOW THERE COULD BE SUCH HOLES IN A PERSON, AND I'M AFRAID I'LL FALL IN … PLEASE, GOD, JUST A TOUCH. OR A WORD. EVEN IF IT'S IN A DREAM." SHE TOOK A DEEP, WET BREATH. "THANK YOU. THY WILL BE DONE, OF COURSE. WHETHER I LIKE IT OR NOT." SHE LAUGHED WEAKLY. "AMEN."

—Brenda, after the loss of her husband, in
Stephen King's *Under the Dome*

MEMORY

God gave us memory so that we might have roses in December.
—James Matthew Barrie

A memory may be a paradise from which we cannot be driven,
it may also be a hell from which we cannot escape.
—John Lancaster Spalding

Every moment and every event of every man's life on earth plants
something in his soul. For just as the wind carries thousands of
winged seeds, so each moment brings with it germs of spiritual vitality
that come to rest imperceptibly in the minds and wills of men.
—Thomas Merton

Memory confuses me.

One the one hand, it connects us with the past; on the other hand, it shackles us there.

Sometimes, we remember things with precision; other times, we remember things as we want to remember them.

Memories are clearly very real—who can deny them?—but a precise scientific explanation of memory has yet to be found. Doctors push parts of the brain to trigger memories, but what are they triggering? Chemicals? Chemicals imprinted with pictures?

Time itself confuses scientists. We live in the present. The past is gone, never to be retrieved. The future awaits; it is not yet actualized. We live in the constant now, book-ended by two realities that feel very real but don't exist. Photographs capture moments that no longer exist (let that sink in).

I have mixed emotions when it comes to photography. I love looking at most pictures, but pictures of my dad? I feel … dishonest, I guess, looking at them. He is not alive. Pictures of him present a person who doesn't exist in a time that doesn't exist. Am I just playing an elaborate game of pretend?

And yet, what would we do without memory? To have no recollection of what has taken place before us; to have no memory of all the things, people and events that have made us who we are—that can't be good either. So I have to have an opinion of memory that balances these two realities.

Memory is a gift for two reasons.

First, it is a gift because it allows us to remember things which exist no more. Because of this, we don't lose our sense of place in the universe, in life, in the overall scheme of things. We need to remember our roots. When the children of Israel left Egypt, God constantly reminded them of where they had been. The first fruits offering in the Old Testament always began with the people saying, "My father was a wandering Aramean ..."

Second, memory is a gift because God said so. Jesus told His disciples that the Holy Spirit would bring all things back to their memory as they wrote about His life and teaching. When God thinks memory is good, then memory is good.

But if the staying power of memory is a good gift, so is the temporary nature of it. If we remembered everything, we would go insane. Our brain is constantly reorganizing, shuffling memories so the most important stay in the front of our minds while the others recede, sleeping, waiting for triggers that may or may not ever shoot them to the front. The Apostle Paul once wrote, "Forgetting what lies behind, I press on ..."

No formula can tell us which memories ought to stay and which ones ought to go. All I know is this: I

> GOD GRACIOUSLY DESIGNED OUR MINDS TO REMEMBER SOME THINGS ... BUT ALSO TO MERCIFULLY FORGET OTHER THINGS, KNOWING WE CAN'T HANDLE ALL THAT HAPPENED BEFORE WHILE DEALING WITH ALL HE HAS FOR US RIGHT NOW. FOR SOME REASON WE INSIST ON TRYING TO PRESERVE EVERY MEMORY VIA PHOTOS, VIDEOS, SCRAPBOOKS, JOURNALS, ETC. I'M THANKFUL FOR THE PRESERVATION OF SOME MEMORIES. BUT REMOVING OR AVOIDING CONSTANT REMINDERS OF PEOPLE WHO ARE NO LONGER WITH US CERTAINLY DOES NOT REMOVE THE SIGNIFICANCE OF THEIR CONTRIBUTION TO OUR LIVES, BUT RATHER ALLOWS ROOM FOR WHAT GOD HAS FOR US NOW.
> —HF

am embracing the memory of my father, but right now I am keeping my distance from the photos. I don't want to confuse my already fallen brain. I want to remember him—that is an unspeakably precious gift. But the fleeting nature of memory is a gift also, and I want that too.

I think of the ghost of Hamlet's father, who could not leave his tortured son alone. I think of the ghost army in *The Lord of the Rings,* imprisoned in Middle Earth. I think of all the ancient legends of the lingering dead, or of all the movies about the dead but not gone (like *The Sixth Sense).* In almost all of these venues, the lingering presence of the dead is a bad thing.

So, I'm letting my father go. He has no unfinished business here. He doesn't need to instruct me in vengeance. I don't need him to linger any more than is natural.

God made my father let go of this world.

He is helping me let my father go too.

FAITH

It is hard to watch the world we know slowly crumble around us.

I remember two distinct thoughts bouncing around in my head whenever I made eye contact with Dad while he was sick: "I cannot watch this happen," and, "I wonder if he knows what I am thinking." Both of those questions caused me to look away. I understand Job a little better now: "My face is foul with weeping, and on my eyelids is the shadow of death" (Job 16:16). My eyelids carried the shadow of his death. I shielded my eyes to hide my soul, and my weakness robbed us both of something important.

It's as Thomas Merton once said, "Death is someone you see very clearly with eyes in the center of your heart: eyes that see not by reacting to light, but by reacting to a kind of a chill from within the marrow of your own life." Those eyes—my eyes—conveyed too much for me.

The chill in my marrow rises so quickly to the surface. Since Dad's death that I have had trouble looking people in the eye, even those I love. Perhaps especially those I love. I fear what I will see in them, and they in me.

The Bible often uses a "seeing" metaphor to talk about our spiritual interaction with God. Ephesians 1:18 tells us to pray that the eyes of our heart will be enlightened so we can know the hope to which we are called. The Psalms tell us to lift up our eyes to see God's provision. Jesus said if our eyes are dark, the darkness is great. Perhaps this is why the Bible tells us to "walk by faith and not by sight." Sometimes our eyes are too dark, and what we see is just too hard to process.

This does not make faith blind. Faith might just be different that we imagine it to be. Perhaps we have read into the Bible a perspective on faith that is not there.

"Faith is the substance of things hoped for, the evidence of things not seen" (Hebrews 11:1, KJV) is one of the most commonly quoted verses about faith. Look at a few other ways it is translated:

Faith is the confidence that what we hope for will actually happen;
it gives us assurance about things we cannot see (NLT).

Now faith is the assurance that what we hope for will come about
and the certainty that what we cannot see exists (ISV).

Now faith is the substance of things hoped for, and the sign
that the things not seen are true (Bible in Basic English).

Now faith is a well-grounded assurance of that for which we hope, and
a conviction of the reality of things which we do not see (Weymouth).

Well-grounded assurance? Certainty that what we cannot see exists? It sounds like faith has more to do with thinking God's thoughts that it does with feelings. It sounds like faith involves reason, and study, and a decision. Contrary to popular opinion, faith has to do with a dedicated firmness in believing what we know to be true, not a nebulous, feel good, emotionally charged euphoria. Faith does not need our feelings as much as it requires our commitment.

Faith is not a power we tap into or manipulate. It is not a tool like the Force in *Star Wars,* where proper use grants us control of the very fabric of the universe. It's not like the world of *The Secret,* where we can change the universe just by wishful thinking. It's unfortunate that so many presentations of faith promote these two ideas: If I can just feel more strongly or "press in to God"; if I can banish all negative thoughts from my mind and words from my vocabulary, God MUST respond the way I want him to, because I feel really strongly that He must.

But faith is not wishful thinking. Wishful thinking happens when we hope American Idol contestants will all have a realistic view of their own talent. Wishful thinking happens when runway models see any type of high calorie food. Wishful thinking happens in

> I'M PERSUADED THAT FAITH AND FEELINGS ACTUALLY HAVE VERY LITTLE TO DO WITH EACH OTHER; YET, I FIND THAT THEY HAVE ONE THING IN COMMON: WHICHEVER OF THE TWO I FOCUS ON SEEMS TO HAVE AN UNCANNY ABILITY TO DISTRACT FROM (OR DROWN OUT) THE OTHER.
> —GJB

Wolverine fans when the University of Michigan plays Ohio State. None of these scenarios captures real faith.

Faith, for a Christian, is a commitment to a God in whom we have good reason to trust. I preached a sermon at church in January 2005, several years after Dad died, in which I said the following:

> *"I can't say that I felt "in love" with Jesus at that time my dad died. I can't say I felt much at all for a while. I remember a breakfast with Karl and Ted, and a trip with Ted and Anne in which I told them, "I don't understand prayer." I did not feel good for a while. But I loved Jesus. We had made a covenant that was still there. I like the "in love" that can be felt in times when the presence of God is so palpable I can almost feel it, and I'm bouncy and shining and smiling and dancing, or deeply moved. I have experienced that, and that's important. But I don't ever want infatuation to overshadow the deep love of a Savior who walks with me when I don't feel like walking at all. I remember talking to Jim, and telling him that I wasn't doing so good. Jim basically said, "I know how it goes. Hang in there." Do the next thing. Go doesn't go anywhere. We made a covenant. Sometimes the reality of a relationship is more important than the feelings that go with it."*

C. S. Lewis summarizes well: *"Faith is the art of holding on to things your reason has once accepted in spite of your changing moods."*

COMMUNITY

A key truth about the Trinity involves the relational nature of God. The Bible says that God is love *("Whoever does not love does not know God, for God is love" – 1 John 4:8, NIV),* and if God weren't Many in the One, His love for Himself would be incredibly narcissistic. But He is not a Cosmic navel-gazer; the love and relationship in the Trinity gives us a model of community.

Discussion of the Trinity can often seem like a tiring theological exercise, so let's ask the big question: Why does this matter? It matters because we are image bearers of God, and our ability to relate to each other bears the image of God's inherently relational nature.

When we live in true connection with others—in openness, honesty, and truth—we display the image of God while simultaneously learning something about Him. Maybe that's why Jesus said that all of the Law could be summarized this way: love God first, and love others as you would yourself. As we love, as we commit to and experience the self-sacrificial, other-centered nature of Christian community, we experience something about the very essence and nature of God. Our families are intended to be the "first responders" to the potential tragedies of loneliness and isolation, but when the family falls short, the second responders are meant to take over.

In the desert of a world that is increasingly fragmented and individualistic, the experiences of true community offer a life-giving oasis of hope and connection. To the extent that followers of Christ can incarnate this community, the world is a better place. Paul Brand has written in an essay called "A Presence":

> *"Jesus departed, leaving no body on earth to exhibit the Spirit of God to an unbelieving world—except the faltering, bumbling community of followers who had largely forsaken Him at His death. We are what Jesus left on earth ... He left a visible community to embody Him and represent Him to the world ... We form God's presence in the world through the indwelling of His Spirit. It is a heavy burden."*

Being the presence of God is a heavy burden, but it is also a crucial one. When my friends Clint and Jolene found out my dad had died, they swung into action. They cooked for our family for the next three days while we prepared ourselves for the trip south; they rented a minivan for my family; they drove with us to Alabama, stopping overnight with us in Nashville; they stuck around a couple of days in Atmore to be close. They gave time, emotion, energy, and emotion, and asked for nothing in return. They know how to bear heavy burdens for the sake of others. They know what incarnation means.

In the wake of Dad's funeral, I didn't always experience—and I choose that word carefully, "experience"—the presence of God in the people around me. I didn't always like community. In fact, I often experienced people simply as a burden.

I experienced people as burdens when their imperfections overshadowed their blessings. How many days did I not want to go to church (or school) because I knew people would look at me with pity, or avoid me, or try to wring conversational blood from a relational stone? How many days did I try to avoid my wife and kids, because I did not want to whine yet again to my wife about how much I missed Dad, or tell my kids that "Daddy doesn't feel like playing"? How many times did I work up a head of steam over my extended family's perceived lack of interest in poor little me?

I experienced people as burdens when they forced me to relate to them. People at church and school who really knew me, who had a right to be a part of my life, did not take "Okay" for an answer when they asked how I was doing. People sent me cards on Father's Day, making me acknowledge that they carried my grief with me. My children wanted to talk about Grandpa; my wife wanted to go on dates so I could tell her how I was really doing; my aunts and uncles called to talk, or invited me over for holidays.

Hindsight may not be 20/20, but it is disturbingly clearer. In hindsight, how did grief have the ability to make such crucial blessings look so much like a burden?

In reality, none of those things were true burdens. People were imaging God and True Christian community for me; I just couldn't see it or appreciate it at the time. In fact, the very presence of this community around me was and is crucial as a vehicle of hope, but it cost them the hard work of helping to shoulder a burden that was too heavy for me alone.

When people around me cared enough to pity me, that was a heavy burden for them to bear. They honored my privacy enough to avoid me; they tried to connect with me in an awkward attempt to be a friend. That was crucial for my journey.

It was a heavy burden for my wife to listen to me (again), and for my kids to (still) want to play with me even if they sensed my distance, and for my aunts and uncles and cousins and friends to love my dad so much that they grieved, too.

The memory of a father, son, brother, and uncle, gone before his time, is so strong that it permeates a reunion years after his death. My extended family does their best to walk this path of loss with me, and they bear this burden though their footsteps are as imperfect as mine.

Ah, for the ability to think and feel about people and events the same way God does. Imperfect blessings are not burdens. Imperfect blessings are the best gifts imperfect burden bearers have to offer on this side of heaven.

I will not let grief have the final word on this issue. Hope will say the last, and it is this: "All errors are covered up by love" (Proverbs 10:12).

PAIN AND HARDSHIP

We must all suffer one of two things: the pain of
discipline or the pain of regret or disappointment.
—Jim Rohn

I will not say, do not weep, for not all tears are an evil.
—J. R. R. Tolkien

I have been contemplating whether or not pain or hardship is automatically bad, or intrinsically evil. Is all pain (or hardship) a result of the Fall, or was it present even in Eden?

Subjectively, death, pain, sickness, and adversity seem obviously evil, a part of a fallen world. I also have moments of objective clarity when I realize that adversity, not pleasure, matures me; that death makes me appreciate life.

I am seeking the discernment to know where the subjective and objective meet. I worry that I will mangle Scripture by forcing it to fit my ideas. I also worry that I will mangle Scripture by not being honest about what is really contained in God's revelation to man.

Hopefully, what follows avoids both extremes.

Classical portraits of Eden show a life free of any possible frailty: there is no sweat, no fat, no thorns, no insomnia, no pain, to anger, no insurmountable obstacles, no hunger, no Michigan football… You get the picture. It's what we thought Disneyland was when we were kids.

But is that really what the Bible says? Clearly, there was a fall from a state God declared "good," and with it at least two levels of fallout.

First, "Sin entered into the world, and death by sin." (Romans 5:12, KJV). Theologians agree this is a reference to spiritual death. Historical Christian theology has stressed the theological implications of this more than the physical.

Second, there was a practical problem: pain would increase in childbirth; now we will toil by the sweat of our brow; now the relationship between the husband and wife will become a contest of wills. The combined language captures the spiritual and physical falling away from a good state to a fallen one. There seems to be an distortion and intensity of already existing conditions, not a total reconstruction of life.

If Augustine is correct, evil is a distortion of the good, a diminishing or falling away from the way things ought to be. Evil does not exist as a separate, contradictory power attacking good. In Eden, everything existed in its intended state. After the Fall, the distortions began, and they continue to this day. The greater the distortion, the more an intrinsically good thing is twisted and distorted, the more evil comes into the world.

Depravation had stormed the beaches.

Here's the catch: I don't think the Bible automatically supports the claim that there was no pain in Eden. I think we have projected our experience of these things in a fallen world into the "good" world. I believe these things existed, but were *in the state they were supposed to be.* The Second Law of Thermodynamics was already in effect, and it rocked. Pain and hardship were unfallen. They were experienced in a different way—a good way, a complete way, in a world in which *shalom* was at its peak.

Shalom is a Hebrew world that means "peace," and it covers peace with God, with each other, within, and with the world. Here's the important question: can pain and hardship be a part of world of perfect *shalom?*

I think it can. The cycle of growth in plants requires the cycle of nature as we know it; for things to grow they need nourishment or fertilizer—something else had to provide that. Decaying material feeds new life. Either there was a state in the garden where everything existed in stasis, or it was a dynamic, living environment. God commanded Adam to "take care" of it; he was to steward a perfect world. Really? What would there be to take care of, if everything was perfect as we traditionally think of it? "Subdue and rule over" suggests a progressive movement—there is some territory to be gained (or re-gained).

I wonder if Adam's world was Edenic in that everything was constructive and purposeful, even difficulties. Would a good life be one in which you never really appreciated a good meal, because you were never hungry? In which you did not learn temperance, because you never got a stomach ache after eating too much? In which you never had the thrill of swinging carefully in a tree, because there was no fear you would fall? In which you never fell into bed at night exhausted but happy, because you had worked hard that day? In which you never had the satisfaction of working our a relational sound, because it was impossible for you to misspeak or act rashly? Was man really at his peak if his nerve endings did not register properly?

Was the Garden of Eden really like *Groundhog Day,* where nothing could ultimately go wrong, so nothing really mattered?

Why do I feel like a desire to return to Eden is a desire for a Brave New Eden?

After the fall into sin, God said Eve's pain in childbirth would increase, not start. He didn't say, "Now men will have to toil"; God said now they will toil painfully "by the sweat of their brow," as if there would now be a toil that did not contain that much hardship before. Adam clearly had his work cut out for him when he was to "subdue" the earth, and only a small portion was good to go. When God talks about the post-Fall relationship between Adam and Eve, He doesn't say that now conflict will start. He seems to say it will escalate as their wills now clash in a manner that is deeply broken, tragically sinful.

I think this distinction is important.

Perhaps one of the aspects of the fall into sin is that now we can't see the big picture; we don't understand the role that pain and hardship play in life. Maybe *shalom* is a life in which there is patience, peace, and hope at the bottom of everything, because it will work out all right. In this life, if you want peace, the storm must at least be possible. In this life, if you want the sweet, cooling oasis of hope, a desert of disappointment has to be near. If you want to learn patience, you might have to wait in a line somewhere behind someone who pays in pennies.

Maybe in Eden, pain was in its *purest form:* it stayed in perfect balance with the environment. Perhaps Adam and Eve did not think of pain as we do today, as something to be avoided at all costs. Maybe pain then was always protective or rewarding—think of how we snatch our hand back from a fire in time because the flames hurt us, or how we push through a strenuous exercise and have a rush of endorphins afterward.

If there was an unfallen state of pain, then the One who gives us "every good and perfect gift" could give us a good gift of pain as well. Like love can be distorted into lust, and kindness can become enabling, good pain can become bad as well.

The Fall *at least* has to do with a loss of our ability to see the big picture and understand the role that the dark threads play in the tapestry. We lost the clarity of the role of pain; the illumination that comes from God and shows us clearly how "all things work together."

So the question returns: was the Garden missing dark threads in the tapestry, or was it a state in which the shadows enhanced the light?

Perhaps some pain is a blessing; perhaps God gives some gifts that we don't recognize.

Lance Armstrong once said, ""Pain is temporary. It may last a minute, or an hour, or a day, or a year, but eventually it will subside and something else will take its place. If I quit, however, it lasts forever."

Lance Armstrong is not the Apostle Paul, but he can still be insightful.

Maybe (among other things) hell is for quitters, for those who do not understand that pain's power is momentary, and its Conqueror is eternal.

Maybe (among other things) heaven is for those who refused to give up; those who turned to the only One who can make the pain last for a moment. More than ever, we rely on His strength to be made perfect in our weakness.

GOD

A little girl was coloring on a large drawing pad when her father entered the room and asked, "What are you drawing, honey?" Without looking up, she replied, "I am drawing a picture of God." Her father smiled and said, "But no one knows what God looks like." Without a pause, she retorted, "They will when I am finished."

There are a lot of people talking about God. Oprah has found the Secret about him. The New Atheists simultaneously explain why God is so evil and why He doesn't exist. Movies portray God as a big pantheistic Tree *(Avatar),* an absent, deistic father *(Clash of the Titans),* or just a mean bully *(Legion).*

This can make conversations difficult. Maybe you meet someone, and both of you have something in common: you believe in God. That could be the beginning of a great discussion, but terms must be clarified. What kind of God do you both believe in? Definitions matter: you might talk to someone who doesn't believe in God, and in the course of conversation, you find out you actually don't believe in that kind of God either.

Here's the big question: What do you think of when you think of God?

God can be seen as a figure on top of a tall ladder. We climb and struggle, but when we get to the top, God has extended the ladder another couple of rungs. God is that inner voice that always says, "That's not quite good enough. You are not quite good enough."

God can be seen as unsympathetic, emotionally distant, cold, and interested only in facts or performance. People who see God in this way ask: "How could God understand my problem? Why would God care about what I feel?"

God can be seen as too busy with important things to care or to listen. Think of a long line of people waiting for God's attention. Now picture yourself at the end of the line.

God can be seen as abusive, as a bully. This is the God who carries a big stick and enjoys using it to control, threaten and punish people if they misbehave.

God can be seen as unreliable. This God, for one reason or another, cannot be trusted. God may be loving one day and unaccountably angry the next. God may make promises, but they won't be kept. God may be weak, passive or unable to provide the help and protection we need.

Some think of a God who abandons. Those who fear abandonment by God may try hard to please God in hopes that God will not leave. Even when He feels close, He could leave at any moment.

Worst of all, some think of God as a Cosmic Abuser, an all-powerful bully who lords his strength over us. He hands out pain in this life, and hell in the next. He is Nietzsche's Superman, and He is consumed by the will to power.

I offer a potentially uncomfortable observation: our relationship with our father heavily influences our view of God.

On the upside, if Dad was great, God seems great. Jesus said of God the Father, "If we ask for bread, will he give us a stone?" and because our dads are good we think, "Of course not. God the Father wouldn't give me a stone. I might even get cake." And if we fathers can be godly dads, our kids are well on their way to having a healthy view of God.

On the downside, if Dad was not great, then we understand what Chris Hitchens means when he says that neither is God. That makes sense. If we fathers damage our children, guess what they will probably think God's plan is for them? You can bet they don't think of the plan God had for his people in Jeremiah 29:11 ("Plans to prosper you, and not to harm you.")

As a pastor, I talk with a lot of people about God. For many, the idea that God is a Father and the church is a family is not a blessing, because their father and their family damaged rather than nourished them. God has a way of showing up in long forgotten or repressed memories.

I preached a sermon once about childlike faith, and at one point I said the following about Vincent:

> MY FATHER ALWAYS HAD TIME FOR ME. HE WOULD LAY DOWN HIS BOOK IN HIS DEN TO LISTEN AND TALK TO ME. IF I WAS SICK, HE'D COME TO MY BEDROOM AND HOLD MY WRIST TO CHECK MY PULSE. ANY WONDER THAT IT'S EASY FOR ME TO TALK WITH GOD?
> —MY MOM

"He can't see my love or understand my strength, but he has seen how they look time and time again. This is why parenting is so important. Children place a faith in their parents that one day they are meant to place in God. We fill God's role for small children; they don't understand God, but they understand us. We are God's ambassadors to children. And when they get old enough to begin to comprehend God, they will apply what we have helped to teach them about faith."

As I reread this entry in my journal—it's October 2010 now—I am again grateful that my dad was a good ambassador. I might not be jumping again yet, but I'm at least poolside now. I'm glad He's patient.

So what do I think of God?

He is big; He is emotionally strong; He stands for truth and justice; He looks out for the downtrodden and the outcast; He loves beauty, and the outdoors, and His children; He asks that we be good, and forgives us when we are not; He is simultaneously demanding and patient. He's glad I love basketball, but He thinks it's just a sport, and he assures me that His love for me does not hinge on my ability to throw a ball through a circle. He would enjoy an evening around a woodstove with me playing games; He might think me childish and immature at times, but will often quietly let me be that way; He tells the angels how proud He is when He sees things about me that have grown up; He loves my mom, and my sisters, and me.

I think God says things like, "Don't carry so much next time" when I burn out, and "Why didn't you tell me?" when I don't reveal to him my struggles.

Well, God, I'm telling you now, and like my father, I believe you love me for it.

> I CAN'T IDENTIFY AT ALL IN TERMS OF POSITIVE CONNECTIONS REGARDING MY PERCEPTION OF GOD AND MY PERCEPTION OF MY FATHER. HOWEVER, AS I HAVE GOTTEN TO KNOW MY HEAVENLY FATHER, MY PERCEPTION OF MY EARTHLY FATHER HAS BECOME MORE BALANCED, ALLOWING ME TO LOVE AND HONOR MY EARTHLY DAD BETTER.
> —KJ

Thanks, Dad.

PRAYER

"Prayer is a declaration of trust. Jesus gave us the model
in Gethsemane, His prayer moving from "Take this
cup away" to "Not my will but yours be done."
—Phillip Yancey

"The disquieting thing is not simply that we scrimp and begrudge
the duty of prayer. The really disquieting thing is that it should
have to be numbered among duties at all. For we believe that we
were created to glorify God and enjoy him forever? ... If we were
perfected, prayer would not be a duty, it would be a delight."
—C. S. Lewis, in one of his "Letters to Malcolm"

Based on Biblical teaching, personal experience, and the testimony of other followers of Christ, I believe there are several things about prayer that we have to acknowledge as Christians.

1) **God listens and acts.** The Bible states clearly that God hears our prayers, and that they matter to Him. *(The earnest prayer of a righteous person has great power and produces wonderful results." James 5:16, NLT)* He does not turn a deaf ear to our pleas and praises; He fully engages with us. He gives us the honor of having an impact on the world through Him. As C. S. Lewis once wrote, "It may be a mystery why He should have allowed us to cause real events at all; but it is no odder that He should allow us to cause them by praying than by any other method." Whether we see the effect or not, God has given us the privilege of being capable of praying prayers that matter.

2) **Prayer is not magic.** Prayer can effect God, but prayer does not manipulate God. *("For we do not know what to pray for as we ought, but the Spirit himself intercedes for us with groanings too deep for words. And he who searches hearts knows what is the mind of the Spirit, because the Spirit intercedes for the saints according to the will of God." Romans 8:26–27, ESV)*

Freud thought we create God as a projection of our wishes, but let's be honest: if God were a wish projection, I am pretty sure He would have to do what I wanted Him to do.

I find this lack of wish fulfillment tremendously comforting, as this limitation relieves me of the obligation of trying to control God based on my force of personality. I cannot coerce or trick God. Any belief about God that obligates Him to me or manipulates Him according to my will does not match up with the Biblical presentation. God does not generate our reality just because we wish He did. If we make God our choice, it does not mean we will get a Rolls Royce—or that my dad will be relieved of his cancer. If we make God our choice, we will get a cross. I am pretty sure that is not wish fulfillment.

3) **The words and the style of prayer do not guarantee results.** I don't have to pray the A-C-T-S model for God to hear me, though the model is fine. I don't have to say, "In the name of the Lord Jesus Christ" to avoid accidentally praying to the wrong Jesus. I don't have to bind and loose things, or get two or three to gather in His name, or invoke the Holy Spirit yet again—though none of these are bad ideas.

I think we sometimes act more like the prophets of Baal than Elijah in the Elijah in the biblical account. Elijah pretty much just prayed; Baal's prophets got increasingly frantic and creative in their attempt to get God's attention. We may not cut ourselves, but I wonder if the money and time we spend in discovering secrets about prayer are not a modern equivalent. If I can just do THIS, I can finally get God's attention.

I'm quite certain He is aware of me—and you.

We can just say "Help" if that's all we've got, and that works pretty good.

4) **Prayer is primarily (though not only) a means to align me with God, not align God with me.** (*"And he said, "Abba, Father, all things are possible for you. Remove this cup from me. Yet not what I will, but what you will." Mark 14:36, ESV)* The direction of "Thy will be done" is from us to God, not vice versa. The prayer of a righteous man avails much because the righteous person prays for an outcome that aligns with God's plan. Righteous people can't manipulate God, but they can walk so closely with Him that their goals become indistinguishable from His.

Here's a hard lesson: God does not necessarily share my view. I am simultaneously annoyed and grateful for this. The childish part of me insists that God think and feel like I do. The adult part of me praises Him because He doesn't.

In spite of all my struggles with understanding prayer, I am praying again, not because I have it all figured out, but in spite of that fact. Slowly, God is rebuilding something within me, and He whispers ever so quietly that He is near, waiting patiently for me to speak and listen.

I am building from the basics: The Lord's Prayer. I am plumbing its depths as I get my prayer legs back under me. Prayer humbles us by reminding us that life cannot be lived by our power alone. I need to pray if for not other reason than to remind myself that I. Need. God.

Our Father in heaven,
Hallowed be Your name.
Your kingdom come.
Your will be done
On earth as it is in heaven.
Give us day by day our daily bread.
And forgive us our sins,
For we also forgive everyone who is indebted to us.
And do not lead us into temptation,
But deliver us from the evil one.

(Matthew 6; Luke 11)

EMBRACING LIFE

"I've read the last page of the Bible. It's all going to turn out all right."
—Billy Graham

"To whom shall we turn? You have the words of life."
—The disciples to Jesus

In October, 2010, I preached a sermon on Jesus' claim to be the "Way, the Truth, and the Life." I really struggled with the "Life," which should come as no surprise after reading this journal. But the sermon prep shifted something inside of me.

While studying the Beatitudes, I realized I was regaining my sense of Life. I am blessed even when I am broken, even when I mourn. Jesus said the Kingdom of Heaven is still mine in spite of my losses, and that He will comfort me. My disappointment is not a result of God's unfaithfulness; it's my distorted view of Him that lets me down. In fact, in the midst of my weakness God manifests himself most clearly and strongly.

Thomas Merton once wrote, "A life that is without problems may literally be more hopeless than one that always verges on despair." A life in which I am forced to rely on God is richer and deeper than a life in which nothing pushes me beyond the shallowness of myself. When the Apostle Paul said he wanted to know Christ, we often quote "and the power of His resurrection," but often forget that the next line is, "and the fellowship of his suffering."

There was a time that I wrote—in one of my more lucid moments—a list of things I needed to remember about life in spite of how I felt:

"That God is good, even when life is not.
That He is near, even when I don't feel Him.
That He is watching, even when my eyes are closed.
That He is not silent, even when I silence him with distractions.
That He is not hidden, even when I cannot see Him;
That death wins one battle with everyone, but not the war."

The Bible begins with a world that is amazing, then transitions into the chronicles of a world that is falling apart in every possible way, and finally ends with a revelation of heaven.

Contained within this panorama are many small stories that shadow the Big Story of all of creation. People are born so cute, burpy, and relatively innocent; people do stupid and sinful stuff that damages their lives and the world around them; they can find forgiveness and new life. We see beauty emerge from ashes; we see mourning become dancing.

Throughout the history of the world, God has patiently shown us that He has the ability to overcome chaos, darkness, despair, and bondage, and bring freedom, hope, and life.

Ultimately, the story found fulfillment in Jesus. All the other stories had been preparing us for this: God became human and conquered death to show us once and for all that He can make all things good. Creation groans and mourns, but it is being redeemed.

That is what the death and resurrection of Christ show us. We who are humbled and broken can one day find ultimate healing; we who are wondering if this life can be salvaged have an answer.

> IN GOD'S UNIVERSE, WHILE WE ARE NOT FREE TO CHOOSE WHETHER WE SUFFER, WE ARE FREE TO CHOOSE WHETHER IT WILL ENOBLE US OR INSTEAD WILL EMBITTER US.
> —DESMOND TUTU

FROM HEART TO HEAD

The Intellectual Side of Pain

In the process of my college studies, I took a class on the Problem of Pain through Trinity Theological Seminary in Indiana.

What follows are some essays from that class addressing the problem of pain and evil from a more philosophical and theological level. Any wisdom found has its source in the philosophers and theologians who are often quoted.

I am including this section for three reasons.

First, there is often a difference between the way things are and the way things ought to be. Before the entrance of sin into the world, life was "the way things ought to be." Now, post-Eden, we live in a world of "the way things are," in all its beautiful brokenness. My journal mostly captures the way things are, at least at that point in my life. These essays are an attempt to address the way things ought to be, from a biblical perspective. To whatever degree the "are" and "ought" overlap, thank God. The journal chronicled my journey; the essays explain my faith.

Second, I have come to realize how my mind stabilized my heart. I knew some things to be true about God, and that knowledge held my heart steady. A belief based purely on experience can be exciting and meaningful, but a faith based just on feelings is too mushy. A belief based on facts can be intellectually satisfying, but a purely factual faith is too cold. The bottom line is that either truth controls our feelings, or our feelings control our view of truth. A well-rounded faith is one in which the heart warms the mind and the mind steadies the heart. My journal recorded what I felt; these essays capture what I believe.

Third, my journal seems to capture a sense of pessimism that does not reflect the life I have today. Maybe it is human nature to be more transparent and honest in the tough times. Whatever the reason, I wanted this book to close in a manner that reminds us that, though we grieve, we have a bulwark of truth to support us and a foundation of hope to sustain us.

Before the essays begin, I am including a brief primer of terms and issues for those who are unfamiliar with the philosophical debate. The primer is just that—a primer—and the essays are not intended to be a definitive statement at all. If you are not interested in what follows, I hope you found the journal helpful. If you are interested, I trust that what follows will be helpful as well.

The Problem of Evil: A Glossary of Terms

The Historical Christian Description of God

God is all good, all knowing, all powerful, perfect and infinite, a person, and triune. Being all powerful (or omnipotent) means whatever is able to be done, or is possible to do, God can do it.

In addition, God is immutable. He does not change in His essence; He cannot gain or lose moral or metaphysical stature. However, He may change in respect to conscious states of God; for example, He speaks and doesn't speak. God's nature doesn't change in time, but He acts in time in ways that change.

Evil Defined

A common belief is that evil is the opposite of good, but what is meant by opposite, and what is meant by good? If God is pure goodness, did evil exist somehow coeternally with Him as a dualistic opposite within His nature or outside of it?

Augustine thought good was interchangeable with being. Insofar as a thing is, it is good. Insofar as God exists, for example, God is automatically good. Since He has infinite existence and being, He is infinitely good.

According to Augustine, evil itself is a *privatio boni,* a privation of good. Evil does not even have the ontological respect of existing. If God created all things, and everything He created was good, then evil is not a thing God created; in fact, it is not even a thing. Evil does not exist on its own; it needs a host. It is parasitic.

Norman Geisler describes evil in basically the same way, as "a deprivation of some good that ought to be there." Cold is the deprivation of heat; shadow is the deprivation of light. Evil is the deprivation of good. Frank Turek, in a blog entry called "Parasitic Evil and Independent Good," gives some examples of this privation definition:

1. *Volition (or freedom) is a good thing, but using it to murder is obviously not. A volitional act becomes an evil act when the act has been deprived of some good that ought to be there.*
2. *Sex is a good thing, but rape is not. Rape deprives sex of a good that ought to be there.*
3. *A sense of self-worth is good, but arrogance is bad. Arrogance exists only because it deprives self-worth of a part of its goodness.*

The origin of evil relates to the Fall. God created everything in its place. Evil takes place when the created being loses that original vision of God and tries to break the boundaries that God has set. Sin entered the world through pride.

Augustine says fallen man is good because he is a man, and by reason of existence he is good. But he is also tainted by evil because his will is fallen.

We are able to sin, says Augustine, because we are created from nothing, which means the tool of creation was in and of itself not intrinsically good. We are beings created from nonbeing, which means almost by definition we cannot be good on our own.

Augustine believed there was a tendency for things created from nothing to return to nothing; we may have been made perfect originally, but we are clearly able to be corrupted.

An evil condition occurs when some person, thing, act, state, or condition is opposed to or exists in opposition to God's holiness, goodness, and nature.

Natural vs. Moral Evil

Moral evils are evils that come about by the misuse of the freedom of some moral agent, specifically humanity. Natural evils are states of pain or misery that occur because some process in nature has gone wrong. Richard Swineburne, emeritus professor of philosophy at the University of Oxford, posits four categories of evil:

Type 1: Physical evils. These are painful sensations, from being burned by a match to experiencing pain from medical procedures.

Type 2: Mental evils. These are things like painful emotional scars (e.g., loss of loved ones, painful memories from emotional abuse, etc.).

Type 3. State evils. These are evils and undesirable states in the world, such as hatred or ugliness (e.g., litter, entropy, etc.).

Type 4. Moral evils. These are evil actions of moral agents with foreseeable or unforeseeable evil consequences of types 1–3. (Alvin Plantinga has attributed natural evil to Satan, so all evil is under the banner of moral evil.)

The Problem of Evil

The Logical Problem of Evil (LPE) says that "God exists" and "Evil exists" are logically incompatible. The Evidential Problem of Evil (EPE) says that while evil does not show God's existence to be impossible, it is evidence against God.

The Problem of Evil is more a declaration of a challenge to the theist: the existence of evil and pain in the world should call into question the existence (or at least the nature) of God. This is not yet necessarily a question of whether God exists, but of understanding why God allows the evil He does.

An Argument from Evil, on the other hand, is an explicit argument from the existence of evil to the nonexistence of the theistic God.

There are two key ways of addressing the problem of pain, evil, and suffering. A defense against the problem of evil attempts to show that God and evil are not logically inconsistent. A theodicy attempts to show that God and evil can coexist, and this claim can be argued in a way that it is both probable and credible.

The Classic Articulation of the Problem: David Hume

Hume developed an argument first credited to Epicurus. If God is willing to prevent evil but not able, He is impotent. If He is able but not willing, He is malevolent. If He is neither impotent nor malevolent, why is there evil?

Hume said there are four problematic conditions upon which all of the world's ills turn, and if God had changed these, the world would be a better place.

1. **God uses pain to move or motivate us.** Why couldn't God have lowered the pleasure we feel? Hume asks why pain is used. His

assumption seems to be that the good life is a life that maximizes pleasure and minimizes pain. (For a more modern version, read the ethics of Peter Singer.) To Hume, the locus of moral value (its goodness) consists in being in a good or pleasurable state.

2. **God controls the laws of the universe, so He could just will that evil be eradicated whenever it is about to happen.** Even a tinkering with the laws of nature that allow entropy, for example, could do away with some of the pain and suffering we experience.

3. There is frugality in regard to how goods in nature are distributed. **God is apparently stingy in giving out good-making properties.** Cheetahs are fast, for example; why aren't we all?

4. **The workmanship in nature appears shoddy.** (Hume is thinking of natural evil, such as excessive wind and rain, or the long line of extinct animals in world history.)

The Role of Possible Worlds

A possible world is simply the way the world could have gone. When we consider our world, our intuition tells us that things might have been different. A possible world is a world that could theoretically and logically exist.

There are some restrictions on these possible worlds. For example, there is no such thing as a possible world where there is a real contradiction. A possible world is one where anything you think of to add is either already included or precluded by what is there already. Of course, only one possible world is actual (this is referred to as the *alpha world*).

On God's Ability to Create a World in which People Always Freely Do What Is Right

Philosopher J. L. Mackie says free will is valued by Christians since we don't want to be robots. Obviously, people sometimes freely do what is right. So, it is theoretically possible that on all occasions, a free human agent does what is right freely. Why didn't God enact this possibility to make a world in which all human agents choose right freely?

Is it possible for an omnipotent God to have created something He cannot control—namely, our free will? Of course, that depends on the definition of omnipotence. (Is an omnipotent being one that can do all things we can think of, or just things that are actually possible to do?)

Mackie claims that since God created the laws of logic, He must be able to break these laws. But theists say that He cannot break or act against the laws of logic, as they emanate from His very nature. God did not create the laws of logic in the same sense that He created the laws of nature. Logic is rooted in God's way of thinking. Breaking them would break Himself.

Alvin Plantinga claims a person is free with respect to some action if the person can perform that action or refrain from that action. A world containing free creatures is much more valuable in God's eyes than a world not containing free moral creatures. If these creatures have free will, they will face morally significant actions in a morally significant way, and God desires a world like that.

Plantinga argues that it is possible that every person has what he calls "transworld depravity." Even though there are theoretically possible worlds in which free people do not do immoral things, these were not logically possible worlds for God to make. Fallen choices would happen in every possible world.

The Best Possible World

Gottfried Leibnitz said that God could have created any possible world. Since He is all good, He is compelled to create the best possible world. This world, then, is the best possible world.

Leibnitz thought the best world has the most variety. Existence is intrinsically good, and if the variety is infinite, the world will have infinite value. Otherwise, it will not be one of the best worlds God could have created. John Hick has responded by asking how this includes a world like ours, with the germs that spread cholera. A world without that would be a world with less variety, but would that not be a better world? Or what about two worlds, one with one more person? Would the more populated world be more valuable to God?

A professor at the University of North Carolina, George Schlesinger, says the solution to this problem of evil lies in the *degree of desirability of a state*. God as creator is within His rights to make us the kinds of beings that He did. The goodness of our life is dependent on the kind of being that we are, not necessarily the circumstances around us.

Christians do not say that the best life is the one with a maximum of pleasure and minimum of pain. The best life is one in which God allows us to freely, often through our own efforts, develop character and humanness. This has been called a soul-making theodicy.

Creation awaits redemption in eager expectation; the world will one day be liberated from its bondage and groaning. God allows the earth to groan not only because of the effects of the Fall, but so that we will work to bring about a community and a restoration of culture.

The Experiential Problem of Evil

Rather than saying the presence of suffering and evil are completely incompatible with the existence of God (the Logical Problem of Evil), philosopher William Rowe uses the existence of specific, intense instances of evil to argue against God's existence. This is called the **Experiential Problem of Evil.**

Rowe's syllogism looks something like this:

Premise: There are instances of intense suffering which God could have prevented without thereby losing some greater good or permitting some evil equally bad or worse. (Specifically, he cites the case of a fawn burned in a forest fire, and a young girl in Washington who was brutally raped and murdered.)

Premise: God would prevent the occurrence of any intense suffering He could, unless He could not do so without thereby losing some greater good or permitting some evil equally bad or worse.

Conclusion: God does not exist.

In other words, if there are cases of unjust suffering, God (at least as He is classically presented) does not exist.

There have been four key responses to Rowe. They are as follows, along with Rowe's responses:

1) "Without evil, we would not appreciate good." We enjoy fair weather because it is nice, but if every day were that pleasant, we would not appreciate those picnic days. Rowe says this may address the presence of evil, but it does not address his point, which is the intensity of the suffering.

2) "God allows evil as punishment or a consequence of sin." Clearly, says Rowe, this does not work for a fawn burned up in a forest fire, and maybe even not for the young girl.

3) "It is the price of free will." Once again, this doesn't apply to the fawn, though Plantinga attributes natural evil to the abused free will of Satan. Rowe says free will could be limited without destroying it, so why didn't God allow the attacker to have free will, just not on that occasion?

4) "Evil produces occasions for moral and spiritual growth." Rowe responds that this does not account for the little girl's suffering. God could have brought about whatever He needed to without permitting that particular suffering.

Rowe's argument is really a form of *ad ignoratium,* an argument from ignorance: since he knows of no reason God could allow these cases of evil, he concludes there must be no reason. Rowe himself has noted that the best response to his argument is one called the G. E. Moore Shift (as G. E. Moore was responsible for it).

Moore's reformulation of the argument is as follows:

> *If God exists, God would prevent any suffering possible.*
> *God exists.*
> *Therefore, there are no cases of unjustified suffering.*

Both arguments use a method of reasoning called *Modus Ponens* (If P, then Q. P; therefore Q). But by shifting the consequent and antecedent (or subject and predicate), Moore shows how his line of reasoning is just as valid as Rowe's.

Another response comes from Calvin College Professor Stephen Wykstra. He says Rowe makes his claim without justification: "appears" to be no good is not the same as "knows" there is no good. Rowe is leaving out the theistic belief that God knows many more goods that are beyond our ability to understand.

The Principle of Sufficient Reason says that nothing takes place without a reason. So when an event takes place, even if it is an event full of pain and suffering, there is a reason why God allowed or caused that to happen rather than some other thing (or nothing).

An Example of a Non-Christian Theodicy

Epictetus, a Stoic philosopher, claimed that in everything that happens, one can find occasion to praise providence. One of his later students said even bedbugs have a good purpose, since they get people out of bed. Even the housefly had a role: it was an agent responsible for germination and cross-pollination in the absence of bees.

Epictetus made use of other word pictures (metaphors) on how God made us and the world. The first is a *banquet*. When sitting at the table, there are many good things coming around the table. These may or may not get to you; as things come, you take what is yours and pass on the rest to others. So goes life.

The next metaphor for life is a *play*. We are called to be actors in a giant drama where God is the director. He calls forth different actors, and we don't know whether our role is large, insignificant, or somewhere in between. God decides our role, and we have to believe that we will be able to play our role without being degraded or crushed.

A Brief Conclusion

There is a sense in which we are called to stoically accept our situation: as Job said, "The Lord gives and the Lord takes away; blessed be the name of the Lord."

And yet, the Incarnation speaks to this issue as well. God's suffering in Christ is relevant to our suffering from natural evil; we find it reassuring that God did not sit idly by and behold our suffering from a distance, but lived and suffered with us. He entered in then, and enters in now, to a world of suffering. He would not allow us to suffer if He did not suffer alongside us.

All of creation groans, but only as it awaits redemption. We can embrace hope, as we believe in the One who entered into this broken world, showed He has the power to make all things new, and offered that hope to us.

The Problem of Pain

(AN ESSAY ON THE PHILOSOPHICAL AND LOGICAL PROBLEM OF EVIL)

The problem of suffering and pain in a world that the theist claims has been created by an all-loving, all-powerful, all-knowing God has become a flashpoint in the debate surrounding God's nature and existence. The argument about the mere presence of evil pushes the limits of human history (e.g., Job), but the escalated horrors of the twentieth century, specifically the Holocaust, have brought the debate about the magnitude of the problem to the forefront now more than ever.

Interestingly, the problem of pain was not an issue that was a serious threat to Christian thought until the last several centuries; suffering has only recently been seen as a ground for final skepticism rather than an incentive for inquiry. When Descartes and other theologians began to discuss the existence of God by stressing philosophy and reason rather than the person of Christ, they opened the door to a new room of argument.

The problem of evil—specifically, the claim that the existence of evil necessitates or at least argues strongly for the nonexistence of God—has been formulated on two different levels. The most foundational question is whether the existence of God and the existence of evil are compatible. A different approach grants that God and evil may exist but questions what kind of God would allow the apparently gratuitous pain we see in the world.

Though there is some variation in the formulation, the logical problem of evil can be stated as follows:

God exists, and is omnipotent, omniscient, and perfectly good.

This is logically inconsistent with the idea that evil exists, because a perfectly good being would want to eliminate evil, and an all-powerful being would eliminate evil.

Evil exists; therefore, God does not exist.

In this scenario, damage is done not only to the concept of God, but to the character of God as well. David Hume (who was more interested in the challenge to the moral nature of God than to His existence) cites Epicurus' famous questions: "Is He willing to prevent evil, but not able? Then He is impotent. Is He able, but not willing? Then He is malevolent. Is He both able and willing? Whence then is evil?"

Alvin Plantinga has been a driving force in pointing out a key weakness: the presence of evil would prove that God doesn't exist only if we add the premise that God does not have a reason for allowing evil to exist. It does not necessarily follow that a perfectly good being would prevent suffering if He could.

Granted, this is not a positive argument for the compatibility of evil and God, but a negative argument that states there is at least not an *incompatibility* with the two. However, other philosophers such as Stephen Davis have joined Plantinga in building on a tradition classically formulated by Augustine: the Free Will Defense.

The Free Will Defender argues that it was good for God to create people who had genuine choices, and whose choices were not coerced. Humans were created to be able to make ethical choices in a morally significant way, and this ability makes this world more valuable than a world that does not contain free action. Therefore, the existence of evil springs from the potential misuse of the good of free will. (Note that this does not claim to have completely solved the problem of whether a choice to do evil has to be one of the choices; it merely notes that the ideas of God and evil are not incompatible.) As a result of the work of Plantinga and others, many, if not most, current philosophers no longer see the Logical Problem of Evil as strong evidence against the theistic God.

However, the sheer scope of the pain and suffering on earth is daunting to the theistic task. In this Evidential Problem of Evil (EPE), the issue is no longer whether or not the existence of pain and the existence of God are compatible; in a sense, their possible coexistence is granted at least for the sake of argument. The issue now has become whether or not the amount of seemingly senseless, gratuitous, and non-beneficial pain is compatible with the existence of a God whose characteristics match those of the God who survived the Logical Problem of Evil.

The core of the EPE argument is that if this world could be better, then the traditional theistic God does not exist. This inductive EPE argument has been popularized by William Rowe in the following manner:

1. There exist instances of intense suffering which an omnipotent, omniscient being could have prevented without thereby losing some greater good or permitting some evil equally bad or worse.

2. An omniscient, wholly good being would prevent the occurrence of any intense suffering it could, unless it could not do so without thereby losing some greater good or permitting some evil equally bad or worse.

3. There does not exist an omnipotent, omniscient, wholly good being.

Rowe cites two primary example to support his argument: a fictional story of a fawn being burned to death horribly in a forest fire, and the true story of a young girl from Flint, Michigan, who was cruelly raped and killed. If there is a God, says Rowe, God is required by His nature to make a world that does not contain this seemingly gratuitous evil. At minimum, says Rowe, it is unlikely that "an omnipotent, omniscient being could not have achieved at least some of those goods (or prevented some of those evils) without permitting the instances of intense suffering that are supposedly related to them." Couldn't God have created a world in which life is even a little bit better?

Here then is the crux of the argument concerning possible worlds. If someone could show that God could have created other, better worlds but did not, the traditional Christian theistic concept of God would be dealt a serious blow.

This concept of possible worlds has generated much controversy. Some philosophers such as David Lewis believe these possible worlds are real worlds, while others believe they are purely theoretical and should be appealed to only for the purpose of illustration. Others wonder how crucial the argument even is, since the argument of apparently pointless evil has lost some of the impact it once had. However, the widespread appeal of the argument certainly makes it worthy of a considered response.

The response to this problem of evil, like the problem itself, has a history. Gottfried Leibnitz popularized the idea of possible worlds when he suggested that in spite of all we see around us, this world is still the best of all possible worlds. His basic argument was that since God's will is perfect, and He has willed this world, then this world must be the best possible world. Something about this world compelled God to create it rather than any other, and that is a good enough reason to believe as Leibnitz does (this is also known as the Principle of Sufficient Reason).

Voltaire strongly mocked him in the classic *Candide,* a story in which the hapless hero undergoes and sees horrific instances of suffering while attempting to adhere to the philosophy of his teacher, Pangloss, who told him that no matter what happened, it was for the best in the best of all possible worlds. When Candide finds out that his childhood love had been killed, he asks if it had been from love sickness. "'No,' says Pangloss, 'she was disemboweled by Bulgar soldiers after having been raped as much as a woman can be.'"

Pangloss goes on to say that he is dying from venereal disease which had been passed on to him through a rather complex assembly of characters. However, he assures Candide that "it was an indispensable element in the best of worlds." As the story unfolds, the hapless Candide sees the worst that humanity has to offer: greed, slavery, debauchery, and cruelty. In other words, says Voltaire, if this world is the best, God has a lot for which to be held accountable.

Since then, many philosophers have agreed: there is not much to be said for an ineffectual God whose excuse is that He always does the best He can. He is stuck alongside us picking up the pieces of history, which are many and bloodied.

This is, of course, a pretty astonishing assumption. In spite of how daunting a task this would be, the claim is that if God allows evil, we humans must be able to understand it, or it counts against God.

So who is right? Is this world the best of all possible ones? The worst? Somewhere in the middle? Are other worlds even possible?

In response to this argument, a number of possibilities have been proposed.

First, would it have been better for God not to have created this world? If He knew that evil would be present, perhaps He should not have created the world; in fact, He may have been morally obligated not to create the world if He knew there would be pain and suffering.

In response, theists have noted the idea of making a moral comparison between No World and Any World at All is nonsensical. Norman Geisler says this is a category mistake, because nothing and something have nothing in common. Comparing a morally bad world and no world at all is like comparing apples and oranges.

C. S. Lewis said comparing being and nonbeing was just a word game, an argument that carried no weight or significance.

To Lewis, the more important issue was the reconciliation of the world as it is with the character and nature of God. So while this possible world seems intriguing as a possibility, it appears illogical as a reality.

A second possibility is that God could have created a world where people freely chose to do good every time they have a choice. Given all possible worlds, there must be at least one world where every person freely chooses to do right every time; hence, this world is not the best. A crucial aspect of this debate is the theory of middle knowledge. This is the idea that God knows every choice in every situation of every possible free creature. The Jesuits called this "middle knowledge," because it was somewhere between God's knowledge of the possible and the actual.

The Jesuit priest, Luis Molina,, specifically, separated God's knowledge into three categories: **natural knowledge, free knowledge, and middle knowledge.** Building from Molina, proponents of the middle knowledge theory argue that God knows what a free creature could do (natural knowledge) and will do (middle knowledge) in any given situation, not because He creates circumstances that causally determine what the free creature will do, but because He knows how the creature will freely choose.

God knows that agent X, placed in circumstance Y, will freely perform action Z. (References in the Bible that appear to support this theory include 1 Samuel 23:6–13 and Matthew 11:20–24, where God provides information about what would have happened had a given situation occurred.)

The atheodicist can use this argument as well. Using this theory as a base, why not argue that God, through middle knowledge, could have brought about people He knew would always choose good? And since He didn't, well, we are back to our original critique.

Alvin Plantinga addresses this issue by submitting his theory concerning **transworld depravity.** If there is middle knowledge, God may have known in advance that significantly free people would always commit at least one wrong action, no matter their world or circumstance.

God could have created a world where no one chooses to do moral evil, but then that would not be a world with free people. Perhaps God has even actualized a world populated by people who, in spite of the horrors that have been committed, make the fewest possible wrong choices in any possible world with free will. Hitler committed some of the world's most horrible atrocities; is it possible that in every other world, Hitler would have committed at least the same amount of evil? And even if Hitler had not, perhaps someone else would have brought about the same horrors, if not more horrific ones.

Robert Adams—who believes universal transworld depravity is implausible—agrees with Plantinga that perhaps God could not create free creatures who would always choose to do moral good. He also does not believe that God exercises middle knowledge, which adds an element of guesswork into God's creation. However, Adams still believes that the existence of free will, which requires possibilities from which to choose, suggest the implausibility of a possible world of human perfection.

In fact, the idea of God creating only people who always freely choose good may in essence take away the idea of freedom.

In a world with true freedom of choice, God cannot actualize a scenario in which free people always will choose good any more than He could actualize a square circle; it is logically impossible. If free will is true and genuine, God cannot make a world that forces a freely chosen decision in a contradictory direction. So once again, while this world seems to be theoretically desirable, there is much doubt that it could be actualized.

A third possibility is that there is a possible world where people are free but must choose good, or (and this is certainly not a desirable world) where people are free but must choose evil. The apparently illogical self-contradiction aside, these possible worlds face the same criticism that faces the "no world" scenario: it is not a good analogy. Comparing a world where there is freedom to a world where there is no freedom is comparing not just apples and oranges, but more aptly apples and nonapples. For example, a world with no free creatures may be better in a physical sense, since it has less pain and sickness. But physical improvement is not the only marker with which to judge the goodness of a world.

If we are to be free to be good, we must also be free to be bad. And while this freedom allows for corruption to creep in, it also allows for goodness, and moral improvement, and hope.

But is this evil worth it? According to the Free Will Defense, yes. Therefore, the possible world under discussion, even if possible, would not be a better world. A world with free people is more valuable than a world with none. God has given people the dignity of being able to choose good or evil. If people choose poorly, their decision is not God's fault.

A fourth possibility is that there could be a world where God would intervene so that pain is lessened or removed. This possible world does not question the presence of evil, but the amount and intensity.

David Hume asks for the eradication of all evil: "In short, might not the deity exterminate all ill, wherever it were to be found, and produce all good, without any preparation or long process of cause and effects?"

William Rowe, as noted earlier, asks for a much more modest intervention: merely the nullifying of gratuitous evil, or evil for which we can see no apparent justification.

John Roth points to what he calls God's largesse in giving freedom that has resulted in a wild world full of gratuitous pain. According to Roth, we have more power and freedom than we can handle.

The primary basis for believing this world is not the best world is the argument that pain is bad, and pleasure is good; therefore, the more pleasure and less pain the world has, the better the world would be. Pleasure evidently has an intrinsic value which is good in itself, regardless of whether it is goal-directed. In a sense, this is a utilitarian argument concerning God's character: a "good" God would provide the greatest good (pleasure) to the greatest number of people.

One problem with this view is that it is difficult to see how one can know that all instances of pain are bad; many instances of pain are good in themselves or lead to a good result. The pain of a shot leads to a vaccination against disease; the discomfort of a strenuous workout leads to better health; the searing pain that tells us our hand is being burned on the stove enables us to prevent further damage.

Indeed, leprosy is such a destructive disease precisely because lepers cannot feel the damage that is done to the body, which results in infections that ultimately lead to death. Dr. Paul Brand, after working in the United

States' only leprosarium, said, "If I had one gift I could give to people with leprosy, it would be the gift of pain."

But what about the pain that accompanies wrong action? Surely God could prevent that. One should not have to suffer because of the decisions of others. Could one even explain how a world like this could actually be designed and exist?

Who can describe the mechanism of creation and the laws which would govern its continued existence, and why should this even be considered? Until this happens, perhaps we should accept that every possible world with sentient creatures similar to ourselves must contain a certain amount of evil, or it would be massively irregular. After all, a world full of constant interruption of natural law to mitigate our bad actions would most likely be a world of chaos. One solution is to have a world without people, but is that really a better world than one with people?

As Lewis points out, there is really no way for God to achieve this pain-free utopian goal without removing free will. The removal of even one negative effect would create a world without that effect, but we would not know this. Since we were not aware that God had already removed maximal pain, God would be put into the same position again. We would demand He remove the next evil effect. Where would this cycle end?

A world with only pleasure would not be a "good" world; its massively irregularity would be as great a defect as the presence of evil. Perhaps God has more important things to do than maximize our pleasure.

This world would also take away the ability to build character, to act nobly and virtuously, and to display courage and temperance and fortitude. The Savage of Aldous Huxley's *Brave New World,* in his defense of life with pain, tells Mustapha Mond, "What you need is something with tears for a change. Nothing costs enough here."

This would be, in Richard Swineburne's words, a toy world in which nothing matters very much. This ability to make moral choices and be rewarded or punished accordingly is a crucial part of the soul-making process, a process which is necessary in the formulation of what makes us truly human.

In an online article entitled "Augustine on Evil," Greg Koukl has noted, "A world that had never been touched by evil would be a good place, but it wouldn't be the best place possible. The best of all worlds would be a place where evil facilitated the development of virtues that are only able to exist where evil flourishes for a time. This would produce a world populated by souls that were refined by overcoming evil with good. The evil is momentary. The good that results is eternal."

From a logical perspective, it may not even be possible for a world to exist that contains only intrinsically good states of affairs, since every state of affairs is of such a nature that every possible world contains either the state or its negation.

A fifth possibility is that the idea of other possible worlds is incoherent, either philosophically or logically.

Is there a possible world where there are no possible worlds? If so, the idea is nullified: if our world has no possible worlds, there are clearly no possible worlds; if there is another actualized world in which there are no possible worlds, then ours doesn't exist.

For reasons such as this, it is not actually clear which possibilities God could have chosen. We have to consider metaphysical possibilities, not just conceptual or logical ones. Conceptual possibility is not the same as metaphysical possibility. Lewis wondered if this was perhaps the only possible world, because the idea that God could have created something else but didn't was too uncomfortably anthropomorphic for him. A God of perfect goodness and wisdom would not need to engage in internal debate.

To Lewis, the idea that God would have ever needed to debate this issue undermines the character of the very God being argued against. But since the existence of God is what is being argued, this should be addressed as a result of the argument, not during the process. If the nature of the God being discussed is destroyed during the process of formulating the argument, the argument may as well be abandoned before it begins.

Finally, getting caught up in speculation about what a best possible world would look like—at least from our perspective—may be an impossible exercise in futility. We can always think of something slightly better.

The "degree of desirability of state," to use Schlesinger's terminology, has no limits. Fans of *Toy Story* laugh when Buzz Lightyear claims he is going "to infinity and beyond," because the concept is absurd; is it any more absurd when applied to theoretically possible worlds?

The sixth possibility is this world, the world in which we live: a world where free creatures can and do sin, and as a result there is suffering. Hume's character Demea argued, as did Augustine (with what has been called the "principle of plentitude"), that in spite of individual cases of suffering, the good of the whole is more important and has been adequately accomplished in the best possible manner in this world. This view sees the universe as an "organic whole," whose value comes from something more than just the sum of the good and bad parts. For example, Swineburne has noted that God could have created three types of worlds: a finished, perfectly good universe that needs no improvement; an unfinished, evil universe that can never be improved; or a good universe that is partially finished, allowing for significant moral actions as our character is built rather than given to us. This partially finished universe has in it an overwhelming, intrinsic good (free will) that completes it and gives it a worth greater than the sum of its individual parts.

One does not have to agree with every point of Augustine's or Swineburne's principles to argue that, given the value of free will, this world is perhaps the best world presently achievable. **This is the *best way* to the best possible world.**

The root of this argument is that free will is of such a great good that the possible misuse of it by free creatures does not require God not to create it. Any world without free will would not be a better world; thus granting free will is the best manner in which to make possible the best possible world.

The core of the Free Will Defense is that, despite His omnipotence, there are many possible worlds God could not have actualized; no matter what God had done, free creatures with the ability to do actions of moral significance may have always done at least some wrong.

This world that He actualized is a world of free will. God, being good, made all things good. One of these good things is free will exercised by rational creatures. Free will is of such an intrinsically good nature that its very existence in a world containing it is better than either a world without it or no world at all.

Though free will does allow for the potential misuse, God is not sitting idly by watching a fallen world destroy itself. God in His mercy is nullifying evils that we don't see (2 Thessalonians 2:6 mentions God exercising restraint upon certain forces in the world). God does occasionally intervene; we may not understand why He intervenes in some situations and not in others, but that is not necessarily for us to know.

Is it possible that God has actually mitigated the circumstances surrounding the evil resulting from free choice far more than we realize? Alvin Plantinga's idea of transworld depravity suggests that in every possible world, free creatures choose to do evil at least once. Perhaps God has actualized a world in which the greatest amount of people choose the least amount of evil. If one accepts the idea of middle knowledge, this would seem to be possible. (The idea of middle knowledge is certainly not decided, but a God without it is not omniscient, which is one component of the God being argued against.)

William Lane Craig goes one step further and suggests that it is possible that people on earth who never accept Christ are people who would not have accepted Him in any possible world. God has actualized the best world feasible within the framework of the "best way" and has chosen the best balance between saved and unsaved.

Of course, the task of understanding evil remains. Sometimes we know a good purpose behind a bad situation; sometimes we know God's purpose. But sometimes apparently purposeless evil exists which we cannot explain. Perhaps God has reasons we do not understand. These reasons would justify the presence of evil if we knew them; unfortunately, we cannot know them. For some, this puts God on the dock because we see nothing that will justify this particular evil.

However, we should expect that we would not have the ability to know and understand all. Our inability to know this does not make our belief in God irrational. The possibility that there are reasons we don't know of is as probable as the possibility there are no reasons at all, so the argument must turn to the background evidence.

Even if one does not understand why evil occurs in the manner and the extent to which it does, theists believe that evil will one day be stopped. It has been argued that an all-good, all-powerful God would want to and could destroy evil; evil is not destroyed; therefore, this God does not exist. The theist responds that there is a distinction between evil not being defeated and evil not yet being defeated. One day, it will be. A God who is wholly good can and one day will redeem evil. As the Apostle Paul noted, creation "groans and suffers" as it waits to be "set free from its corruption" (Romans 8:21, 22).

Part of that redemption, to the theist, is the belief in adequate compensation for suffering after death. The Apostle Paul wrote, "Our present sufferings are not worth comparing with the glory that will be revealed in us" (Romans 8:18, NIV). Revelation 21 speaks of a day when God will wipe away tears and do away with death, pain, and mourning. Are those who argue that nothing in this world can compensate for suffering truly in the position to know? Have they experienced this or spoken to someone who has? Perhaps the testimony of one who has died and come back would suffice—which, of course, the Christian believes has happened in the person of Jesus Christ.

Having looked at the various arguments for possible worlds, one scenario seems not only possible but also probable from a theistic perspective. God chose to create a world in which free will could be exercised: a comparison to No World is incoherent, and the existence of a world of free will is a good greater than its absence or any misuse that may result from it. Through His middle knowledge, God actualized a world in which the greatest number of people would choose the greatest amount of good and the least amount of evil. Possible worlds where there is less pain and suffering are certainly theoretically imaginable but not practically achievable. The presence of free will has made this world the best way to achieve the best possible world—a world in which free will has been obtained because it is of such great intrinsic good that its absence or its actualization in any other form would have been a far lesser good; a world in which the effects of evil have been mitigated to the greatest extent an all-loving, all-powerful, all-good God could do; a world where evil will ultimately be defeated.

Of the many excellent resources out there, these are the ones that most directly guided this paper.

Intellectuals Don't Need God, by Alister McGrath.
Evidence for Faith, edited by John Warwick Montgomery. Essays include "The Problem of Evil," by John Hare.
The Evidential Argument from Evil, edited by Daniel Howard-Snyder. Essays references are as follows:
"Pain and Pleasure: An Evidential Problem for Theists," by Paul Draper.
"The Problem of Evil, the Problem of Air, and the Problem of Silence," by Peter Van Inwagen.
"Some Major Strands of Theodicy," by Richard Swineburne.
"The Inductive Argument from Evil," by William L. Alston.
"Defenseless," by Bruce Russell.

The Problem of Evil, edited by Marilyn McCord Adams and Robert Merrihew Adams. Essays referenced are as follows:
"God, Evil, and the Metaphysics of Freedom," by Alvin Plantinga.
"Hume on Evil," by Nelson Pike.
"The Problem of Evil and Some Varieties of Atheism," by William L. Rowe.
"Middle Knowledge and the Problem of Evil," by Robert Merrihew Adams.
"Soul Making and Suffering,' by John Hick.
"The Defeat of Good and Evil," by Roderick M. Chisholm.
"Divine Goodness and the Problem of Evil," by Terence Penelhum.

Encountering Evil, edited by Stephen T. Davis. Essays referenced are as follows:
"Free Will and Evil," by Stephen T. Davis.
"A Theodicy of Protest," by John K. Roth.

Dialogues Concerning Natural Religion, by David Hume.
Bake Encyclopedia of Christian Apologetics, "The Problem of Evil," by Norman Geisler.
Candide, by Voltaire.
The Roots of Evil, by Norman Geisler.

The Problem of Pain, by C. S. Lewis.

Mere Christianity, by C. S. Lewis.

Introduction to Philosophy, by Norman L. Geisler and Paul D. Feinberg.

Brave New World, by Aldous Huxley.

Evidence for God, edited by William Dembski and Michael Licona.

"No Other Name: A Middle Knowledge Perspective on the Exclusivity of Salvation Through Christ," by William Lane Craig.

"Do Evil and Suffering Disprove the Existence of God?" by Michael Horner.

"In Defense of Pain," by Phillip Yancey.

"Are There Possible Worlds?" by Michael Huemer.

"Augustine on Evil," by Greg Koukl.

Paul and the Problem of Pain

(A CHRISTIAN RESPONSE TO THE PROBLEM OF EVIL)

The reality of suffering is possibly the greatest challenge to the Christian faith. Perhaps that is why the Christian religion, arguably more than any other major world religion, is engaged in a philosophical struggle centered around the problem of pain, evil, and suffering. While Hinduism and Buddhism, for example, view pain as an illusion, an obstacle to be overcome through the correction of the mind, Christianity believes that pain and suffering is very real, and as a result must develop a theology that gives it a coherent framework.

Because of this, Christianity is faced with the difficult task of embracing the reality of evil and making it compatible with the existence of God as portrayed in Scripture: all-loving, all-powerful, all-knowing, and all-good.

Christianity has attempted to deal with this problem on a number of levels. For opponents who have attacked the logical incompatibility of God and evil, theologians have developed a logical counterattack. From Augustine to Plantinga, the argument has been developed that the existence of God and the existence of evil are not mutually exclusive; their simultaneous existence can be reconciled. This defense has apparently been successful, as the Logical Problem of Evil (LPE) has fallen from the high status it once held.

Other opponents have argued that the amount of evil, not the mere presence of it, argues against the existence of God. If there are any cases at all of gratuitous evil and pain, then the God as portrayed in Scripture cannot be real. This Experiential Problem of Evil (EPE) has created a more emotional argument: as one examines both large scale atrocities (the local tragedies one reads about in the local paper), the pervasiveness of pain and suffering seems overwhelming.

The Christian response to this has been to develop different responses that would explain why the goodness of God is not compromised in the face of evil, even evil that is apparently unredemptive in any fashion. Perhaps good things such as free will more than compensate for the pain experienced during life; perhaps, as in John Hick's appeal to mystery, there are unknown goods that make up for the suffering we see; perhaps there will be a system of rewards and punishments in place after this life that will adequately provide a framework in which one will see the justice and love of God vindicated.

Scripture provides numerous examples of followers of God trying to reconcile their belief in a perfectly good, loving, and powerful God with their circumstances: Joseph, who was sold into slavery before languishing in Egyptian prisons for years in spite of God's very personal interaction with him; David, "a man after God's own heart," who spent years of his life on the run from a homicidal king; Job, an extraordinarily godly man who lost everything; and the disciples of Christ, all of whom faced considerable persecution.

Defenders of the Christian faith have developed articulate explanations, or theodicies, to justify the way of God to man. A theodicy, rather than being a mere defense of the compatibility of God and evil, seeks to proactively show God's reasons for allowing evil to occur. And even though Scripture allows one to peer into and analyze the issue of pain, Scripture often seems less concerned with the defense of God's character than with the development of individuals as they seek to handle the difficulties in life. Rick Rood calls this the religious or emotional aspect of pain, as opposed to the philosophical or apologetic: rather than question the existence of God because of the presence of pain, the religious aspect of the Scriptures helps the believer whose faith is tested by trials. Both proponents and opponents of Christianity agree: in this life, there will be pain.

But in moving from a defense to a theodicy, God steps out of the dock and mankind steps in. The question moves from, "What kind of God could allow this to happen?" to "What is the proper way for me to view instances of suffering and pain?" We often expect God to meet us on our terms; from a Scriptural perspective, we are required to meet God on His terms.

Job, for example, experiences a horrific run of events in his life that certainly appear to be largely inexplicable and unfair. Job's initial response? "The Lord gives, and the Lord takes away. Blessed be the name of the Lord" (Job 1:21). The next verse notes that in spite of his situation, Job did not charge God with wrong. When Job eventually does seek to question

God, God responds, "Who is this who darkens counsel by words without knowledge?" (Job 38:2). Job's response shows that he has returned to his initial position: "I have uttered what I did not understand, things too wonderful for me, which I did not know ... I repent in ashes and dust" (Job 42:3–6, ESV).

In the Book of Psalms, King David frankly and poignantly records his odyssey with God, from green pastures to the valley of the shadow of death. However, throughout situations that threaten his life and shake his faith, David always makes the crucial turn as he remembers what he knows of God; he sees God's hand in all.

> How long, O Lord? Will you forget me forever? How long will you hide your face from me? How long shall I take counsel in my soul, having sorrow in my heart daily? How long will my enemy be exalted over me? ... But I have trusted in your mercy; my heart shall rejoice in your salvation. I will sing to the Lord, because He has dealt bountifully with me (Psalm 13, NASB).

The New Testament records a similar situation with John the Baptist. While in prison, John asks, "Are you really the Messiah we have been waiting for, or should we keep looking for someone else?" (Matthew 11:3).

To paraphrase, John was asking, "If Jesus is the Messiah, why am I still in prison, under the world's oppressive posers?" Jesus' reply is similar to God's response to Job: "Go back to John and tell him about what you have heard and seen—the blind see, the lame walk, the lepers are cured, the deaf hear, the dead are raised to life, and the gospel is being preached to the poor" (Matthew 11:4–5, NLT).

In other words, said Jesus, do you believe that I am who I say I am? If so, trust me. While many authors and books throughout Scripture address the problem of pain, perhaps no one explicates it more than the Apostle Paul.

Paul's teaching on pain and suffering is arguably the most broad and in depth of any of the teaching in Scripture, and well might it be:

> Are they laborers of Christ? I speak as a fool. I am more: in labors more abundant, in stripes over measure, in prison more frequently, in deaths

often. From the Jews five times I received forty stripes minus one. Three times I was beaten with rods; once I was stoned; three times I was shipwrecked; a night and a day I have been in the deep; in journeys often, in perils of robbers, in perils of my own countrymen, in perils of the Gentiles, in perils in the city, in perils in the wilderness, in perils in the sea, in perils among false brethren; in weariness and in toil, in sleeplessness often, in hunger and thirst, in fasting often, in cold and nakedness (2 Corinthians 11:23–27).

We are hard-pressed on every side, yet not crushed; we are perplexed, but not in despair; persecuted, but not forsaken; struck down, but not destroyed (2 Corinthians 4:8–9).

To the present hour we both hunger and thirst, and we are poorly clothed, and beaten, and homeless. And we labor, working with our own hands. Being reviled, we bless; being persecuted, we endure; being defamed, we entreat. We have been made as the filth of the world, the offscouring of all things until now (1 Corinthians 4:11–13; previous quotes from NKJV).

Paul was certainly qualified to discuss the problem of pain, though Paul himself does not appear to see it as a problem in the sense that today's philosophers do. As a result, Paul's discussion of pain and evil is far more of a theodicy than a defense.

There are three core theodical types. **Metaphysical theodicies** discuss evil by pointing out that it is inevitable because "evil is an axiomatic corollary of the act of creating itself." **Free will theodicies** cite the existence and misuse of free will as the explanation for evil. **Greater good theodicies** argue that God permits or brings about certain things for a greater good that could not have been achieved otherwise (think of the soul-building theodicies of Irenaeus or John Hick). Paul's theodicy, a type of greater good theodicy, begins with the assumption that an all-good, all-loving God has reasons that we either know or do not need to know.

In fact, Scripture never assumes that God must explain to us why He does what He does. In Romans 11:34–35 (NIV), Paul says, "Who has known the mind of the Lord? Or who has been His counselor? Who has given to God that God should repay Him?" In Romans 9:20-22 (NKJV),

Paul asks, "Who are you to reply against God? Will the thing formed say to him who formed it, 'Why have you made me like this?' Does not the potter have power over the clay, from the same lump to make one vessel for honor and another for dishonor?"

Paul trusted God absolutely in the face of evil despite his lack of understanding. God has proven Himself in many ways. Why would Paul abandon his beliefs in God in the face of difficulty? Rather than make the character of God adjust to fit his preconceptions, Paul adjusted his views of the ways of God.

Though God does not need to explain Himself, Paul clearly did have knowledge of some ways in which God can use pain to bring about an often unexpected good in the lives of those involved.

First of all, Paul notes that pain can build our character. Paul said that, as a Christian, he died every day (1 Corinthians 15:31). This is where "tribulations work patience, and patience experience, and experience hope" (Romans 5:3–4, AKJV). This "blessedness of waiting for our salvation" is important as it brings about a godly change of character. God conforms us to His image through suffering.

The pain that accompanies suffering can do a refining work in us. For example, when Paul struggled with his "thorn in the flesh" (2 Corinthians 12), God used this to stall the natural movement toward pride by allowing hardships and persecutions. From this perspective, the presence of trials is something to be embraced because of the refining work it does within us.

The presence of trials can also allow us to give proof of the sincerity of our faith, as well as purify it. The Apostle Peter talked about genuine faith enduring fiery trials (1 Peter 1:7), and Paul provided a prime example of one whose faith had been tested. 2 Corinthians 11 documents that Paul's suffering gave him the genuine mark of an apostle.

Even natural evil has the potential to remind us that "it's not about me." William Alston argues that "it takes away a person's satisfaction with himself. It tends to humble him, show him his frailty, make him reflect on the transience of temporal goods, and turns his affection towards other-worldly things, away from things of this world."

In the end, the main reason suffering occurs is the main reason everything occurs in our Christian life: to mold us more into the image of God.

Second, pain and suffering develop in us a desire for relationships, both with God and others.

The presence of suffering gives us the opportunity to have compassion for others, to "weep with those who weep" (Romans 12:15). This can be seen in the life of Jesus, who "withdrew to a lonely place" to mourn a loss (John 11:34), was filled with anguish (Matthew 26:38), and was acquainted with grief (Isaiah 53:3). Perhaps that is why Psalm 34:18 says He is "near to the brokenhearted." He cares for us (1 Peter 5:7) because He has been there. Paul rejoiced in his sufferings because they were "for the sake of the body, which is the church" (Colossians 1:24). They enabled him to comfort the troubled by passing on to them the comfort he received from God in the midst of his trials (2 Corinthians 1:4).

God gives us the opportunity to be wounded healers, as was Jesus. Our suffering enables us to more fully "bear another's burdens, and so fulfill the Law of Christ" (Galatians 6:2).

Pain and suffering also force us to look beyond ourselves and see our need for other believers. Paul uses the analogy of the body in 1 Corinthians 12:26–27 (NASB): "And if one member suffers, all the members suffer with it; or if one member is honored, all the members rejoice with it. Now you are the body of Christ, and members individually."

In Ephesians 4:16 (NKJV), Paul talks about "the whole body, joined and knit together by what every joint supplies, according to the effective working by which every part does its share, causes growth of the body for the edifying of itself in love." There is the good of helping others; there is also the good of being helped.

While pain does play a crucial role in our contact with others, it also reminds us that we live in a fallen world full of sin. To borrow some of C. S. Lewis's terminology, this megaphone of pain continues to remind us of our fallen nature, but this is not a cause for alarm or disappointment. This message will benefit us as we are forced to acknowledge the strength of God as He works through our weakness.

Without this reminder, it would be far too easy to live an easy life autonomously, forgetting who we are in relation to Christ. After all, we will not even begin to surrender self-will when everything is going well. Paul noted, "For you see your calling, brethren, that not many wise according to the flesh, not many mighty, not many noble, are called. But God has chosen the foolish things of the world to put to shame the wise, and God has chosen the weak things of the world to put to shame the things which are might; and the base things of the world and the things which are despised God has chosen, and the things which are not, to bring to nothing the things that are" (1 Corinthians 1:26–28, NKJV).

In other words, the greatest work of God is done through fallen, frail vessels—as seen by the world. In the eyes of God, this brokenness, which allows the acceptance of His power, is an opportunity for the manifestation of His glory as He empowers the individual and displays His glory to a watching world.

Through suffering, we learn clearly our need for God. As Paul said, "We also are weak with Him, but we shall live with Him by the power of God toward you" (2 Corinthians 13:4, Douay-Rheims Bible).

There is a third benefit to this awareness of our world of sin and suffering: it can help us focus on the life to come. "This world is not my home," rings the old hymn, "I'm just passing through." What reminds us that our citizenship is in heaven if not pain?

Paul said that living this life with Christ was good, but dying and being in His presence was better (Philippians 1:21). Considering the litany of painful experiences in his life, one can hardly blame him. The idea of a life of reward after this is not frightening; it is meant to comfort those in trials (1 Thessalonians 4:13–18). We do not see life as dust and shadows, here and gone, with no redemption possible after the harshness of life. "Do not lose heart," said Paul, "for our light affliction, which is but for a moment, is working for us a far more exceeding and eternal weight of glory, while we do not look at the things which are seen, but the things which are not seen. For the things which are seen are temporary, but the things which are not seen are eternal" (2 Corinthians 4:16–18, NKJV). The promise of future compensation gives us not only hope for the life to come, but also motivation for living a life pleasing to God. As Paul notes, "Our present sufferings are not worth comparing with the glory that will be revealed in us" (Romans 8:18, NIV).

Augustine wrote, "If there were no resurrection of the dead, people wouldn't think it was a power and a glory to abandon all that can give pleasure and to bear the pains of death and dishonor; instead, they would think it was stupid."

Finally, suffering and pain can allow God to "make known the riches of His glory on the vessels of His mercy" (Romans 9:23; 2 Corinthians 4:7). Psalm 119, for example, shows that in the midst of trials David was humbled and awed as he acknowledged God's provision, prevention, purpose, providence, and protection.

Sometimes the majesty of God only becomes obvious as we see Him work all things, especially evil, to His purpose. Romans 8:28 (NIV) says, "And we know that in all things God works together for the good of those who love Him, who have been called according to His purpose." For example, after Joseph was sold into slavery, he told his brothers years later, "You intended to harm me, but God intended it for good to accomplish what is now being done, the saving of many lives" (Genesis 50:20, NIV).

This presentation of Paul's theodicy is by no means exhaustive, but then again, neither are Paul's reasons. Paul himself acknowledged the "depth of the riches and wisdom and knowledge of God. How unsearchable are His judgments and how inscrutable His ways!" (Romans 11:33, ESV). Though God has revealed a tremendous amount of His character and wisdom, by no means can we expect to grasp the depth or immensity of the ways of God on this side of heaven. The potential goodness of specific instances of pain may not seem easily matched to the reasons listed above, and one should not expect them all to be. However, we have hope that one day they will be understood. Now, we see life dimly, as if in a mirror. One day we will know fully (1 Corinthians 13:12).

While theologians and philosophers will certainly continue Jacob's tradition of wrestling with God for answers, Paul reminds us of several important things:

While God is under no obligation to satisfy our intellectual curiosity, and while God's sovereignty must be embraced, He does not mind our questions. He is big enough to handle the depth and force of our doubts. He will always be holy, just, and good, no matter our circumstances.

One day, a groaning creation will find its redemption in Him, but until then, we trust and persevere.

Of the many excellent resources out there, these are the ones that most directly guided this paper.

Intellectuals Don't Need God, by Alister McGrath.
Apologetics to the Glory of God, by John Frame.
The Problem of Pain, by C. S. Lewis.
The Evidential Argument from Evil, edited by Daniel Howard-Snyder. Essays referenced are as follows:
> "Some Major Strands of Theodicy," by Richard Swineburne.
> "The Inductive Argument from Evil," by William L. Alston.
> "Aquinas on the Sufferings of Job," by Eleonore Stump.

The Problem of Evil, edited by Marilyn McCord Adams and Robert Merrihew Adams. Essays referenced are as follows:
> "Middle Knowledge and the Problem of Evil,"
> by Robert Merrihew Adams.
> "Soul Making and Suffering," by John Hick.

Encountering Evil, edited by Stephen T. Davis. Essays referenced are as follows:
> "Free Will and Evil," by Stephen T. Davis.
> "An Irenaean Theodicy," by John Hick.

Belief: Readings on the Reason for Faith, edited by Francis Collins. Essays referenced are as follows:
> "Faith and the Problem of Evil and Suffering," by Desmond Tutu.

"Good and the Problem of Evil," by Gannon Murphy.
"How Can a Good God Allow Evil?" by Rick Rood.
"A Plan and Purpose in Our Pain," by David Legge.
"Apostolic Suffering," by Barry D. Smith.
"The God of All Comfort," by Lehman Strauss.
"A Good Reason for Evil," by Greg Koukl.

"I read Learning to Jump Again *straight through—except for the times I had to stop and wipe away the tears. Refreshingly honest, Anthony's insightful and winsome writing style helped me process some of the emotions of my own father's death twelve years ago. I hope this fine book finds its way into the hands and hearts of millions dealing with death and the grief that accompanies it."*

Nick Twomey, Founding/Lead Pastor, Bay Pointe Community Church, Traverse City, MI. www.bponline.org.

"An unusually candid account of a man of faith wrestling with God through the death of his father. Anthony Weber brilliantly articulates the raw realities of being enshrouded with grief and the struggle to get beyond."

Jacquelyn Kaschel, National Christian Counselors Association, Master of Letters in Religion and Society; Counseling, Oxford Graduate School; Mlitt, PNH1 (Parelli Natural Horsemanship Level 1), CEIP-MH (Certified Equine Interactive Professional-Mental Health.

With crystal candor, Anthony Weber seems to have strapped a camera to himself as he took a plunge into grief. His personal journal "Leaning to Jump Again" not only offers raw footage of emotions, questions, and doubts, but also deep insights about genuine faith and trust. It dares us to be honest with ourselves and God, reminding us that, no matter how far the drop, how terrifying the fall, how deep the plunge, and how murky the water, God remains caring, capable, and very near.

Gary Bower, Author, "There's a Party in Heaven!"

CPSIA information can be obtained at www.ICGtesting.com
Printed in the USA
BVOW011047130911

271099BV00002B/5/P